MW00899789

DETERMINATION
THE LEGEND OF THE NAKED COWBOY

By
Robert J. Burck II

Foreword & Conclusion by
Todd Rubenstein

Edited by
Constandina Savvenas

Photo Credits
Anthony Ruiz, Jim Richards & Rick Day

First Edition

© 2010, Naked Cowboy Enterprises
All Rights Reserved

ISBN 978-0-557-96468-0

Foreword

Naked Cowboy
Born Robert John Burck
December 23, 1970
Cincinnati, Ohio

As a Record Producer, I often travel to Los Angeles & New York from my Nashville base for executive meetings with Record Companies and other industry related circumstances.

While in New York City some years ago, an artist that I was producing; Dawni & I were walking in Times Square when she suddenly gasped and said: "Oh MY GOD, The Naked Cowboy!!!" She then began dragging me in a direction towards an island where Naked Cowboy was standing, surrounded by onlookers with cameras and people anxiously awaiting their opportunity to get a picture with the New York City Icon.

I had seen him on TV and had seen lots of pictures of people on myspace with him, but I had never really paid it any attention. When Dawni's chance to step up for a photo with him arrived, he said in a humorous and sarcastic tone; "Step up when your ready, your uncle won't mind taking our picture". I shot two pictures, one of the front and one of the back and we laughed & I forgot about it as we headed towards a restaurant where we would be meeting an executive from Atlantic Records.

After arriving back in Nashville from several awesome recordings at Legacy Studios and encouraging meetings with Atlantic Records in New York City, it was time for me to upload pictures from our trip to Dawni's Myspace for marketing purposes. My dear friend and hit songwriter; Buck Moore dropped by my office and I was drawn off track to discuss a song that he had written ten years back called "Nothin' To Do With Love".

Moore has literally had hundreds of songs cut by major label artists and scores of huge hit songs, but this song was one that he wrote as a fun piece to share with his constituents when pitching songs. It starts off with a great story, sounding like something you'd hear from someone like George Strait or Garth Brooks... Then the first line of the chorus changes the face of the song... well, let me share the lyrics of the first half:

Every woman I go out with,
Is looking for a permanent thing.
They, at least, want a commitment,
If they can't get a ring.
Well, I'm just a good old Country Boy,
Looking for a little fun.
But they can't settle for anything less,
Than everlasting love...

But what's wrong with just fuckin'?
I mean some good old fashion humpin'...
Some moanin' & groanin' til the sun comes up
What's wrong with just screwin',
And gettin' right down to it?
What's wrong with just fuckin'
That ain't got nothin' to do with love?

Needless to say, everyone loved the song, but nobody had enough guts to cut it. It quickly became the number one song within the songwriter, artist and industry A&R community in Nashville. So, Moore & I agreed to find an artist and release the song independently... We just had to find an artist who could be so bold as to cut the song and not be afraid of what the industry might think... then I stumbled upon the Naked Cowboy pictures from our trip to New York City. The epiphany unfolded.

I went online and found www.NakedCowboy.com and called the number on the front page. It was Naked Cowboy's cellphone and he answered: "Naked Cowboy". I asked; "Is this the Naked Cowboy fella from Times Square?". He replied; "That would be me". I then asked him; "Can you actually sing?" He uttered back aggressively; "Of coarse I can sing"!

After discussing the possibility of having him come to Nashville to cut the song, we agreed to a unique, one-song record contract. I didn't know what kind of person I was dealing with, he could be a psychopath or just unable to fully complete the mission and possibly not have the responsibility to fulfill my requirements.

Naked Cowboy came to Nashville and we recorded the song. I was originally going to cut the song exclusively at my studio; TMR Productions, but then I received a call from Dan Mitchell at the Tracking Room (the world's best recording studio) and he said: "I hear that you are getting ready to cut a song on Naked Cowboy". I said; "Yes, we're cutting Nothing To Do With Love". He had heard the demo of the song many years back and like everyone else, absolutely loved the song. He asked where I was planning on cutting it and I told him at my place. He then said; "I'll give you the Tracking Room for free if you cut it here".

We tracked the musicians on the song at the Tracking Room and took the music tracks back to my place to complete Naked Cowboy's vocals. This is where I start calling Naked Cowboy, "Robert". We became really good friends. His discipline and diligence drove him through completing the recording and ultimately we made a fantastic version of the song that we ultimately released. We remained in touch and decided to do an entire album called "What The Naked Cowboy Wants To Hear" to release on I-Tunes exclusively for digital distribution.

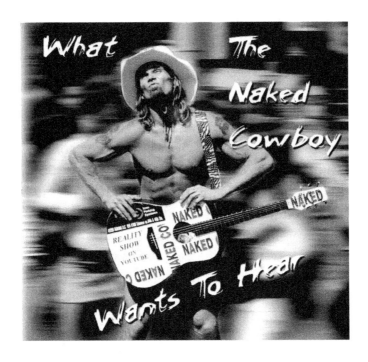

While working on the album, Robert recognized my attention to detail, my connections, business expertise and he offered me an opportunity to negotiate some upcoming business opportunities for him. I agreed and closed two of the three deals. The two deals amounted to the biggest deals that Naked Cowboy had ever experienced. It made sense that we form an alliance and ever since, we have been associates with a common alliance. We formed Naked Cowboy Enterprises and began a journey towards the continued growth and success of this already world recognized brand known as Naked Cowboy.

The following stories mark the era prior to my

opportunity to manage Robert's career and they show how one man's determination can lead him to profound heights professionally and personally. I hope that you enjoy it and find it to be one of the most motivational stories of success that you have ever read.

The Legend of the Naked Cowboy
By Robert John Burck

Introduction

The village of Greenhills is a greenbelt community-trees surround it on all sides. Growing up here always seemed safe and secure and the woods provided my friends and I with countless things to get into. We built forts out of dead logs and buried them under pine needles. We started huge fires in the garbage cans at the campgrounds. We fished, ripped the claws off of crawdads, you name it, and we did it. Everything we did was unsupervised and that made it all the more enjoyable.

My friend, Dan Nolan, and I probably began to play together sometime around the age of twelve. Dan and I both had older brothers who were also friends. In fact, their relationship is probably what brought the two of us together. Dan and I spent the majority of our time together in the creek behind his house that separated the Park Road from a fair stretch of woods. We would pretend we were lumberjacks and would scale trees and anything else we thought lumberjacks would do. Dan's older brother, Sean, was a real lumberjack though. He would go out into the woods, not only with my brother, but also by himself. He'd go out in the middle of the night! He wasn't scared of anything, and he could climb any tree in no time. He made all sorts of incredible stuff too. I swear he could build a log cabin in an hour. One that would look like the real thing, and he was the luckiest guy I knew. He found arrowheads all the time. Real arrowheads and spear heads too. I'm talking about the actual ones the Indians used many years ago. We would just be walking through the creek bed and wham, he'd have another one. I looked every time I went to the creek until I was exhausted from looking, and he told me the same thing every time. "You won't find one if your looking for it." Well I can tell you I never found one despite looking my entire childhood. It would not be an exaggeration to say that I spent forty percent of my youth, on my hands and knees, digging through rocks and gravel, desperately trying to find a damn arrowhead. When I graduated from Greenhills High School I immediately attended a small community college - Raymond Walters. I took all sorts of general courses that one usually is required to take in their first two years of college. In my second year I found myself in a geology course that proved to be a lot of fun. We went on all sorts of little "digs" where we would search through different layers of geological time in and around the city of Cincinnati. We also had independent projects that we had to do from time to time outside of class. On one such project I found myself back in the old familiar creek bed that I spent so much time in as a kid. I never once thought about arrowheads as I searched for several different fossils that were depicted in my textbook that I had brought with me. I hadn't been in the creek bed more than five minutes, in an area I knew like the back of my hand, when I looked down and picked up the first colored piece of nothing that I saw. It was an arrowhead. I couldn't believe it! I instantly thought about how Dan's brother Sean always told me that I'd never find one if I was looking for one and he was so right. Well, I spent the rest of the day looking for another one anyway. I never have found a second one.

Chapter 1
The Illusion

It was July of ninety-seven. I was basking in the California sun in the Palm Springs desert. Believe it or not I was working diligently on my "Hollywood movie career." At least that's what I call it, and since I live exclusively in my own reality, that's what it was. A good friend, and at the time, actively involved theatrical agent, Sid Craig was hosting my little brother and I to a weekend in paradise. I had won a contest in my hometown, Cincinnati, from a local radio station that got my brother and I on a hit T.V. series, "Baywatch."

I went with the expectation of getting a lead role as a lifeguard but we served simply as extras for about two and one third second. Sid, whom I had met several years ago in previous travels to California, had invited me and my brother to extend our two-day trip into a week, and furnished us with a Hollywood studio apartment, a car, food, and a Palm Springs get away. Not uncommon for me as I have always found it difficult not to have such amenities where ever I travel. Reason, well, I'm a most grateful guest who makes it a point to be a professionally trained, inspiring-as-all-hell representative of the human race. Do you doubt me, well then, have me over. Anyway, we were pool side and Sid, who sympathizes with my long range goals for Stardom leaned over towards me on his raft and said, "Robert, have you ever considered taking some singing lessons to develop your speaking voice?" My little bro and I had a most enjoyable time and as I can remember, it was probably the most time I'd ever spent with him. It was a bonding experience that will last a lifetime, making the trip three times as constructive as would have been otherwise. I know now- as I did then, that I created a wonderful sequence of memories and motivations in the life of Sid Craig and my brother, while learning, as I constantly do, what it takes to be a "star in my own life" as Sid once told me I was.

Upon returning to Cincinnati, I re-evaluated my long term and short term priorities. It's something I do daily. Like always, I had planned, determined, accomplished and then wondered what the hell for. I know that I'm better for it. I know that because I'm a stickler for growth and improvement I have created a new circle and reference for my life and everyone else I had contact with. I also know that I have put another national vibe of my personality across the cosmos. I just want more and so I ask what is the next thing that must be done to continue on towards my destiny as the "most celebrated entertainer of all time"? On August 9, 1997, I stepped into the halls of Paul McCready's voice studio. He said I looked like an "action figure." He had me do some la la la's and some he he he's as he accompanied me on the piano. This was to be an evaluation to determine if I had promise. He determined that I could be a good singer if I could make the sounds he coaxed out of me on purpose. I took that to mean that I had the most incredible voice he'd ever heard and that I would make singing a headlining career beginning at that moment. We set up an appointment for my first official lesson and I sang at the top of my lungs the whole way home with the radio- something I'd never ever considered doing before. I guess I never sang along with the radio cause I wasn't planning to be a singer and it would have been a waste of time. After several hours of la la la's and he he he's and now some added ooh ooh ooh's at home for days on end with weekly lessons, I wanted more. I went to my mother's and got her beat-up old acoustic Yamaha guitar and began strumming chords I'd learned from having a few guitars when I was probably sixteen, maybe seventeen. At a time, just before frequent juvenile court appearances had forced me to sell them to pay fines, I played guitar quite a bit. I got music from my father who I remembered singing old Neil Diamond and Beatles songs and old time favorites while playing his guitar. He had the words with the chords printed above them. I knew chords and I knew the melodies and if I had the words, I knew all I'd need was practice. Very simple, anyone could do it.

I took a leave of absence from Fridays where I was waiting tables and learned the guitar to the extent I needed to. Over a period of three weeks I practiced ten hours a day.

Day one through four were very exhausting and frustrating. From then on I could sing and play at the same time and was presentable enough to sing "Bobby McGhee," by Janice Joplin, "Take it Easy," by the Eagles, "Little Pink Houses," by John Mellancamp, "Simple Man," by Lynard Skynard, "Maggie Mae," by Rod Stewart, "Margaritaville," by Jimmy Buffet and "Friends in Low Places," by Garth Brooks. It wasn't my father's music, so I had to get the concept of singing and playing with his music and then transpose what I'd learned to music I liked even more and felt would be more appropriate for me to sing. That's why it took me so long to get a list of songs down, roughly forty hours. Oh yeah, I sucked, but I could get through them and that was all I needed for step two of the performance plan which was to go out and fuck up as much as possible for as many people as possible to get good. I played for family members, gas station attendants, fast food and convenient store patrons and workers. I went back to work at Fridays and played for co-workers and guests. I exhausted the ears of countless people, some of whom I knew. Every time I sang, everyone looked down. No one seemed to be comfortable with the fact that I was horrible and didn't care. I kept telling them, don't feel bad, I was even worse than this! Two months had passed since I began my first singing lesson with Paul and unlike everyone else, Paul said that if I sang for a decision maker in Nashville, "I probably wouldn't be thrown out of the office." I took that to mean that I needed to transfer to a Fridays in Nashville and display my vocal talents with the cover tunes I'd learned to as many Nashville decision makers as I could find. Nashville incidentally came into mind as a result of a friend who worked at Fridays with me who constantly raved about going there to be a famous singer.

It sounded plausible and since she'd never followed through, I considered her role to be a spiritual guide telling me to go immediately. My love life consisted of a princess named Mindy, who had for over four years then toughed out every act of disrespect, dishonor and failure a headstrong egomaniac could put forth. She, much to my resistance, was becoming my foundation for the strength I believed would only come as a result of the fame I am destined to master. I told everyone I knew, and no one was surprised, that I would be leaving for Nashville to be a famous country singer the following day. It was October 27, 1997.

I'd already been geared up for some weeks in cowboy hats and boots and at least by appearance, I looked like the coolest thing to hit the fan since shit. I remember writing words for what I conceptualized as being a possible song called "Going to Nashville," the night before leaving. I also remember my neighbor, Dan, who I hadn't seen in a while, saying as I ran past him towards my car to leave for Nashville, "Robert, you can't just put on a cowboy hat and boots, grab a guitar and go to Nashville and be a famous singer." I left anyway.

Chapter 2
The First Time I Wore Underwear

It was cold and dark the night I first arrived in Nashville, October 28, 1997. I pulled off the interstate and took an exit that sounded like "mid-city." First guy I saw I pulled over and asked if he knew where I could find a TGI Fridays. Five minutes later I was in my new work place talking with the general manager, Ali, and the following day I began work after spending two hours filling out all of their work manuals. I mingled and networked through the servers and after two days of sleeping in motels just outside of town I began staying at another server, Mark Donnelly's, apartment. He was cool and lived only two or three miles outside of work. His apartment served as a haven for many of the servers who just sort of hung out over there smoking pot and drinking and doing what a lot of people I've met over the years do after work, nothing. I worked out each day at the Centennial Park Sports Complex and went out all through the day learning my way around and asking questions. I found out about the "singer/songwriting sessions" that went on somewhere in or around the city every night. Everyone I met knew someone who knew someone who could easily make me a "star" over night. This is just another way of saying they all knew I was obviously a "star" and that with their "limited" to "absolute no" experience, could get me to where I already was. I got grounded at Fridays and made certain that everyone I met knew me as what I sought to accomplish. Jogging through Centennial Park at the week's culmination I ran across a man sitting on a park bench with his acoustic guitar. I stopped and asked him point blank, "how can I become a famous country singer?" He just looked at me seriously and said "to be a singer, you've got to have a real fire in your belly." He mentioned that the average staying time in Nashville was "seven years" for success, and that was contingent upon finding a reputable songwriter who would give you his/her songs to perform. Hence the reason that Nashville is a "songwriting town." It's all about the songs and who's lucky enough to sing them. Tenacity and networking and fitting into the clique. Everyone could sing. Oh, except me. Which left me with nothing but a preponderance of determination. I decided that the discussion meant that I needed to go home, write my own damn songs, learn to sing and perform them, and come back as what I would call a "complete package." The night before my departure from Nashville I went to a karaoke bar with Mark and some of his friends. Looking like a total star, as I usually do, I graced the room being continually approached by onlookers who asked, "are you going to sing?" No one could wait. When I was finally called up to sing, I was drunk and bombed like hell. The song wasn't even in my range if I could sing. Everyone told me I did fine, but I can assure you, it was sympathy. I was excited as all hell though, and tried to sign up again but it was too late. I thought, I knew what I'd done wrong and could fix it all up. Anyway, I just wanted to sing for a crowd without nerves, and I did that. I couldn't have given two shits, really, what it sounded like. I'd done what I'd sought to do. When we got back to the apartment that night I wrote and put music to my first song "Closed my Line." It was about coming home to the one I loved and it only took about twenty minutes to put together, completely. Easiest thing I'd ever done. I knew I could write songs too. I got home and went to Mindy's apartment first thing. She lived in the same small town as me now and when arriving home from any sort of long separation, we'd live in perfect unity and love for at least a couple of days before "goal-oriented fever" would set in. At least that's how I put it. Actually I was still, just being so damn determined to make some sort of amazing example for the world to emulate, that I ignored the one closest to my heart. I wrote twenty-five songs over the next thirty days and had them ready to be performed. I found that to be something at which I am a natural- performing. Most everyone I'd seen sing would close their eyes and go into their own world. I make up stories and then tell them to my audience. They might not sound good, but I'm thinking entertainment, and entertainment is really about communicating, and communicating is mostly visual.

All along I was thinking, hey, if I got cool stories, and look cool telling them, people will like them. I guessed radio would be a problem I'd deal with later. So I went out and bought a sound system to perform with. I made sure it was grand enough to perform at a major sports coliseum so that I wouldn't have to come back and go through the shopping procedure again. I booked myself in every bar surrounding my hometown that would let me in. It was easy! Every club I visited said, "we'd love to have you." They assigned me a date and I showed up. Sporadically family and friends came to see me, and Mindy came every time. Then the problem occurred. I showed up and I sucked. I performed at the "Wooden Horse," "DeJaVu Lounge," "Little Ditty's," "Back Door," "Back Porch," and "Bombay Bicycle Club," once! At most of them I only got in one set before being asked to get out. The manager at the "Bombay" was really nice; the rest were like pissed off at me. I did get much better though through the process. I learned by going straight into battle how to fight, and, that again, was my objective. I took my hard earned experience and flew to Venice Beach on December 23, 1998. I had made arrangements with a friend, Charles Worthington, to stay at his place in Hollywood. He took me to and from the airport and gave me rides to Venice Beach each day. He was the photographer who shot me in Playgirl Magazine, on a previous California trip. I wanted to get to Venice Beach because I knew I could perform for an audience each day without being told to leave, and I knew that I could experiment and determine what I could do to make people pay attention and like me for God sakes. I performed on December 24, 1998 for over six hours in jeans, boots, hat, and loosely fitting flannel shirt with the sleeves cut off. I made one dollar and two cents. The dollar was thrown in by an elderly lady who clearly felt sorry for me, and the two cents was thrown at me. When Charles picked me up after day one, he realized that I was a beaten man and told me not to give up. He suggested that I try something different like "hell, Robert, play in your underwear," laughing, "that'll make em' stop." The next morning I took the bus to the Boardwalk. Charles said he would be down to get me by five, which would give me a total of about eight hours. I first went to the "pit" to work out, you know, "Muscle Beach," then I went to perform. Charles had said when I left that he would bring his camera down and get some shots of me playing. Much to his surprise when he got there I had a guitar case full of dollar bills as I sang, danced and banged out tunes on the guitar in my cowboy boots, hat and underwear. He laughed and smiled like a satisfied old wise man and took a series of photos, as did hundreds of on-lookers. This had been going on for several hours. I got on the news and was a big hit. Charles was so pleased. I remember being driven back to his home, exhausted. He said, "Robert, you have passion, and that's all it takes to be a singer." He then laughed again and said, "my little naked cowboy". See, I knew I could sing.

Chapter 3
Untitled

Two months of straight closes at Fridays as a waiter is enough to put anybody under. Thankfully I'm not just anybody and it doesn't bother me a bit. I'd been practicing like a madman each day singing, and as a foundation for living, I work as hard at the gym every day, period! I knew I wanted to return to Nashville to give it another go with a better prepared version of what I'd only taken as a spectator on my last trip out. Mindy and I were living in love when I returned from Nashville only a couple of months earlier, but that came to an end as I broke from my nightly habit of ending up at her doorstep. I really wanted to go there because it felt so much like home, but I just didn't practice six hours a day, get a good workout and work ten hours at the restaurant when I did that. She didn't have a problem with me working so hard, I think I just felt guilty because I wasn't giving her the attention she deserved. My foolishness created a pattern where we'd go out for two weeks, then separate, without words most of the time, for two, sometimes more, weeks. I would pretend to myself that our four year plus relationship wasn't that important when in fact it was the only source of connection I've ever really had to a fulfilled existence. The excuse I would use was that I had higher obligations to humanity, which I humbly admit that I do, but she I somehow consistently forgot was my favorite human.

March 1, 1998 came along and I was back on my way to Nashville. I remember driving down the interstate singing at the top of my lungs. I had made tapes of my twenty-five songs and played them the whole way. I believed as I do and always will that a star was on his way to make it big, real big. I checked into Fridays again and then a motel outside of town. My friend Mark, who'd I'd stayed with last time out, had moved, making it too wacky to stay at his place. I developed a routine from the day I got there and spent nine doing it. I worked at the restaurant each morning, then went to the Centennial Sports Complex to work out, checked the paper listing I'd found for "singer/songwriter night," then camped out and waited for my turn to sing. Everything I had was in my car and at days end I'd check into a motel , practice, jog, go to bed and do it again the following day. Waiting to sing was a long process that quickly became obviously ineffective. These "singer/songwriter night's" hosted by a different bar or club each night gave nobodies a chance to be somebody among nobodies. You'd show up, put your name on a list and wait till you were called. I went to nine of them and saw damn near the same crowd of people each night. The audience and the performers were the same people for the most part and the people who'd been doing it the longest, played first and left when they had had enough. I went dead last each night and played for the host and the bartender, maybe two or three others who decided to get drunk and couldn't leave. I did play the Bluebird, and that is a

30

nice place. I had an audience of maybe close to one hundred. It was the last place I'd played. I had gone there a week earlier and got my name on the list when they told me that they were full that particular night. I felt that I was well received but again, even at a more upscale, serious place, I don't think the crowd consisted of anybody important. It was more than clear to me that the way to become noticed in Nashville wasn't by singing in these holes. In fact, I remember saying to myself that I had as good a chance in Cincinnati, singing in my closet in my apartment. There, at least, I wouldn't seem desperate, or misguided. Well, maybe misguided.

Back in Cincinnati, I got back to the drawing board. I wrote songs twenty-five through fifty, worked out harder than ever, which of course, is what drives one's ability to operate at full capacity. I'd been promoted to the bar at Fridays and was causing quite a stir there. The bar manager was also my training partner at the gym from time to time and so he got to know me as I was and not just as I was performing at work. I work hard at Fridays, but, I do things as unstructured as imaginable. I never really learned the corporate routines that drive the usual promotional itinerary. Management, outside of my friend, wanted a permanent, more conforming worker who would serve to keep the bar staff looking like management hopefuls. I just wasn't the general manager's suggested appointment and so my days were numbered regardless of the job I did. I did however still seek to prove to be a great worker and sought not to disrupt a steady stream of attendance before taking off on any far reaching, speculative ventures in distant lands. Mindy and I were on again, off again, in terms of our living arrangements and the time we spent together during this period, however, off again was only a physical separation. I could never let Mindy out my heart despite any claim to be self-sufficient and self managed for long. On May 5, 1998 I got an idea. Hey, doesn't the David Letterman Show tape out on the streets in New York sometimes? I wanted to get on the show and the "underwear thing" was on my mind. I wasn't working the next two days and so I took a Greyhound to New York City late that evening. I arrived the following morning. I bummed around til 2:00 P.M., and then went over to the Ed Sullivan studio. I waited until the crowd gathered outside and then got into my outfit. I had two or three pictures taken and then security for the studio came to me and said, "what the hell are you doing?" I told them I was there for the Letterman show as was signified by the word "Letterman," airbrushed on my butt. I was then told to "get my pants on and leave the area." I went down to Times Square and did the same thing. It was at that time that Times Square security came to me and told me to "put on my pants and exit the area." I went back to Port Authority and took another Greyhound home to Cincinnati. Round trip, forty-six hours.

John Robert Burck came about on May 11, 1998. It

was our first day in the T-Bam studio. My brother Kenny, and friends Rick Rieman, Kurt Meulenhard and Carl Shivener worked for eleven days putting down the tracks and mixing our first C.D. which was called the "Small Town Crusader." Mindy shot the cover in front of the Greenhills Branch Library giving it that small town look. We were so in love again, as was always the case when I took the time to realize it. The band and I had been practicing for some time in my brother's basement and I think we were all excited about making a CD. We recorded in Todd Buck's basement and probably prepared the best C.D. ever in light of the fact that we'd only practiced for a period of weeks. We also put it all down, the music, in about four hours. Several hours were spent mixing the tracks in addition to this, but I'm confident in saying that no artist ever seriously intended to make a finished product C.D. in four hours. I had one thousand CDs pressed and began giving them to everyone who asked-even selling a couple. My brother Kenny sold about fifty, which I thought, was incredible. My due date to become the "most celebrated entertainer of all time" had lapsed by one day before receiving the one thousand c.d.'s. I quickly made another challenge. I would become the "most celebrated entertainer of all time" in a year or less. That gave me another year, but now, the idea of it seemed far less ridiculous. It's not about failing if I don't make it. It's about setting a goal grand enough to ensure the maximum drive and effort to get me flying, fast, in the direction I was committed to going. I sent the C.D. with photos and cover letters to every entertainment attorney, independent record label and major record label listed in the "Recording Industry Source Book." I was following a strategy I put together from reading a number of books; "Everything You Need to Know to Make it in the Music Business," "Nashville's UN-written Rules," and "This Business of Music," none of which I know the authors cause I threw the bastards out when I never heard anything from anybody. I took that to mean that the books were ineffective. Kind of like the time I went to my little brother's house and the scale was in a thousand some odd pieces on the floor. He'd been trying to gain weight and claimed the "damn thing wasn't giving him the results he was looking for." This sort of rationale, I can assure you, works like a charm. I've broken several scales, even ones in fine facilities, and I swear I have put on some damn good weight over the years. My next plan was much like the first without the need for anybody's assistance. It was to get material, which I certainly had, but still to get more. For me this means simply, to create songs, and then to communicate them with awesome precision. Get noticed. I figured, hell, if I can't find someone with the capacity to get me famous over night, I'll get famous over night by my own damn self. All I need is a vehicle. It was with this mind-set that I began contemplating what had been effective in the past and what would more than likely work now.

Chapter 4
Opening the Floodgates

 It was September 17, 1998 when I left again for Hollywood. I had the opportunity to shoot for a number of magazines through my photographer friend Charles. It wasn't only an opportunity to shoot, but the opportunity to get to California with a purpose. When on a "get famous with shoe-string resources" plan, it is always best not to leave unless you've got at least one sure thing going. While traveling through California, this time, I got several things accomplished. To begin, I shot for four magazines, though I don't know which ones they were and I've never seen a photo as of yet. I got paid several months later which is how I know they were published. Models rarely get paid before publication. All photography was as usual, nude, but clean, and of course, solo. I also did a video which I believe was called the "Wild World of Naked Sports." It was an experience to say the least. Twelve grown heterosexual men, possibly one gay, shooting baskets, kicking soccer balls, and running for miles at Dry Gulf Ranch in Camarillo, California. It was as hot as holy shit outside. The sun was blasting. Every last one of us had blood-shot eyes from the sunscreen and sweat dripping off our foreheads over countless takes of ridiculously cheesy directing. It was only money I was working for, but, I learned a great deal just by being present for an experience I'd not have had otherwise. It was twelve hours of work, two days straight. I met close to twenty people and have made meaningful contacts that I now have the opportunity to converse with, and encourage, monthly. I'm sure all of the guys were there for money as well as they sought, and still probably continue to seek, to make some sort of lasting career in the entertainment business. More importantly, this trip to California began to create for me a more identified association between myself and the persona I'd only touched upon as of yet, the Naked Cowboy. While at Charles' place, in Hollywood, I went to the Boardwalk again, two days straight, before leaving. I performed as the Naked Cowboy both times and made considerable money, under the circumstances, and got hundreds of photos taken. I was recognized and approached by many that knew me from the one time I'd done this before, a while back. I made the decision then and there, that if nothing was going gang-busters with "John Robert Burck" by the years end having sent hundreds of press packets and CDs out, I'd be the Naked Cowboy in "99!" The universal laws, being as they are, began to create a number of great opportunities for the Naked Cowboy.

I declared, conceptualized, and so the cards began to fall. I placed an ad in Everybody's News in Cincinnati. It read, "John Robert Burck" appears as the Naked Cowboy, wearing hat, boots, guitar and underwear." The date was October 23. 1998. The purpose, to state my intentions in publication. I began to play out with the band as the Naked Cowboy, but only briefly as I quickly recognized that being in underwear took all of the focus off of the music. This made the performances, I feel, not entertaining, but confusing. I also quickly realized that the amount of people who seemed to be talking about the Naked Cowboy was incredible. I sent videos out to the national daytime talk shows and got on the Jenny Jones Show in Chicago, first on November 13, 1998, then on December 6, 1998. I later got an appearance on the Gong Show in California on December 14, 1998. I was received as a sort of "funny goober," but I was received. I got national exposure, which, according to the patent office in Washington, allowed me to use the "Naked Cowboy" in commerce in all fifty states and abroad. That trademarked my new persona. Throughout this period, Jim Knippenburg, with the Cincinnati Enquirer, wrote several articles about me as I updated him. I went to each and every local radio station, in underwear, and got on the air singing and talking about my formulating ideas. I played in front of the Hustler store in Cincinnati in the December snow and got on two local news channels as well as the Trisha Macky Morning Show. It was while being interviewed by her that I came to the realization, "hey, I could do appearances like the one in front of Hustler anywhere in the country, even the world." My second C.D., titled, the "Naked Cowboy" was nearing completion and so I began to formulate a strategy for getting around the country and maximizing publicity/attention. Home-life for me was very serious throughout the end of the year. I was working at Fridays for ten-hour shifts most nights. I competed in a natural bodybuilding show, the Natural Midwest States, to fine-tune my physique, and I was practicing and writing songs like a madman to improve my entertaining abilities. I spent very little time with Mindy or my family with the belief that I just had to honor my duty of making my dreams a reality. I would set the example without regard for personal conveniences or comfort. Sheepishly I ignored the fact that these were the most important elements for making me a man capable of achieving the outcome I am destined to fulfill. No, "it was work or pleasure and I choose work." I was held up and supported by the size of my goals, the pace at which I was moving towards them, and the constant, consistent recognition and encouragement I received from everyone who filled my presence. Point blank, if you work like a warrior, your results will be huge and everyone will honor your progress and stamina. Everyone will be encouraged, and you will make men proud by your level of God-given responsibility to create original acts. Any application of circumstances that does not facilitate such a scenario is foolish and mis-applied. However, if you forget to care about the ones who clearly love and support you the most, are you really honoring such a creed?

Chapter 5
The Tour

I had made up my mind. I will leave today and get
famous. It was Tuesday, January 5, 1999. I wanted to
get to California and back with as many places as I
could in between. I had an 8.5x11 map of the United
States and a pretty good sketched out map of the cities
I thought I wanted to hit. I drove to Nashville, went
into the Blue Grass Inn, called the news and then went
outside in front to play guitar in the freezing cold for
roughly forty minutes. Many people came out of the
neighboring shops but then went back in because of
the cold. I then went to Fridays on Eliston Place,
where I knew people from my previous trips to
Nashville. I called the news again and played in front
of Fridays. By the time the general manager came out
and told me I had to go, Channels Five and Four
interviewed me and so my first city was a success. I
drove to Chattanooga immediately from Nashville and
didn't get there until dinnertime. It was dark and cold.
I made quick friends with the people in a place called
the Electric Submarine. They called the news and I
got a full interview, in depth, a free meal and great
news coverage. I stayed at a Days Inn just outside of
Atlanta that night and had a great workout in the hotel
owner's personal free-weight exercise room. I went to
bed positive and sure of success. On Wednesday I
woke up and drove into Atlanta. I found the city's
main Planet Hollywood and played out front until I
was told to leave by the manager. I then did the same

across the street in front of the Hard Rock Café. I then went on the opposite corner of both that had an empty building in front of it until the police came and put me in the back of their car while checking my license. I had every corner packed with people as they waited to see what would happen to me. I was released and told I needed a permit to play. I got out, went all over town to check outs permits and found that it simply wasn't a ten-minute routine as the police had told me. I went back to Hard Rock and started over again, this time simply not playing the guitar but walking around. The Channel 11-news team came out and then I began to play the guitar. I was invited then, inside the Hard Rock Café where I played on a mini-stage while patrons just stared. The general manager who was unaware of my presence until that point then removed me from the restaurant. I drove to the outskirts of Jacksonville and got a motel. On Thursday, I hit Jacksonville and got a fabulous response, the best yet. I was in the middle of the city and the office buildings poured out with people who watched and took photos. Channel 3 covered me and then one policeman out of fifty or so brought the event to a sudden halt. He was personally offended and acted ridiculous. My job was complete though and so I cooperated. People surrounded me at the back of my car where I passed out remaining CDs, signed Fridays' shirts, and Naked Cowboy Tour Guides. I then drove and got kicked out of Daytona twice by the same officer. Then got on the news without any problem in Orlando. Previous trips to Miami allowed me the privilege of free accommodations at a friend's house near Southbeach where I crashed for the night. I drove to the city of Miami on Friday. It is a huge city. I hadn't even been aware of it's existence. I hit a parking garage and then came out as the Naked Cowboy with no planned place to begin. I just started walking down the busy streets causing lots of attention as I searched for a place to play. I quickly had a cop on my back who called the sergeant to decide on my "o.k." or not. When the sergeant did arrive, there were, at that point, some twenty officers present and hoards of people. The sergeant approached me. I put out my hand and said, "hello, sir, I'm the Naked Cowboy." He looked back and said, "no Naked Cowboy in my town." I was then escorted to my car and made sure to leave the city. I then drove three and one half-hours to Key West. The longest, most boring piece of road I'd ever seen after the first ten minutes. I played on the main drag on the Keys for four solid hours. I got no news coverage cause they have no news coverage. But I did get seen by thousands of people who took photos, and the police could have cared less. I returned to my friend's house in Miami and slept well as I was tired as all hell from a very long day of boring driving. Saturdays and Sundays, I found, weren't good days for Naked Cowboy tours. The cities are empty and no one is around to react to anything. I drove through the entire state of Florida and really couldn't wait to get out. It all looked so much the same it began to irritate me. I worked out hard over the weekend in YMCA's along the way and brushed up on my tan. I read like a crazy man and made lots of calls home to give reports as to what was going on. I continued to live on canned-goods from the back seat as I had been doing since my departure from Cincinnati. When Sunday night came along I was just outside Baton Rouge, where I slept at a rest stop reading my Anthony Robbins book "Unlimited Power."

Journal Entry on Sunday, January 10, 1999

1. How many people can I inspire to achieve their goals by continually focusing and achieving mine?

2. How great will it be to know beyond a shadow of a doubt that not only have I carved out the life that I was committed to, but that I also served as a catalyst for others to do the same. People that I truly love and care deeply about? How many people will also be inspired by these people and then their people? The processional effects of following, without hesitation, ones dreams/destiny cannot be underestimated.

3. Every time the Naked Cowboy succeeds, everyone whom I reach succeeds.

4. Not only does everyone who sees me on the street get a laugh (positive state change), but countless thousands of viewers of the news. Everyone who knows my plans and expectations will be elevated by my efforts. I can truly make a difference each and every day.

5. People receive money, affluence, success, assets, love and all that life has to offer, in proportion to the service with which they provide for others. If I continue to focus solely on how much I can give, how much of my God-given abilities can I accentuate? How much can I unfold myself as the miracle that I am? If this is what makes life pleasurable to me, what

financially could I possibly be worried about? There is nothing that I won't give to make my life and what I stand for a manifest reality. It is a law then that I do have at my disposal; all that life has to offer. Perhaps it might seem as though I don't have "everything" I could ever want, but currently, nothing is stopping me from giving. That's what I want. Life is a process, a journey. As I go I will find ways to give more, to reach more. Every resource I could ever use to contribute on an international level is within me. What a feeling it is to know that the secret of living is giving.

On Monday, January 11, 1999 I drove to Baton Rouge and called Mindy. I'd been thinking of having her meet me in California, via plane, and spending a week of the tour possibly with me along the coast of California. She'd never been to California and felt one, that she would love it, and two, that I would love to have her with me. Kenny Beck, who did my make-up on my previous trip to California, doing the video, would be in Las Vegas working, and sent me the keys to his place in Hollywood. It was a great opportunity for Mindy and I to escape together in the midst of what was becoming a long, lonely time apart. While she thought about it, I went into Baton Rouge and got news coverage from Channel 9 and Channel 2 in front of the Downtown News building. I then drove to Lafayette where I got the news again in front of a furniture store. There it was Channel 3. I also got a newspaper interview before being ushered out of town by the police. I then drove to Beaumont Texas and got on the News, then to Houston where I played for several hours, calling the news without success. Getting on the news in three cities in one day still felt like failure as I reclined into a hotel room outside of Houston. Mindy confirmed the trip to California and I vowed to get Houston with a second attempt in the morning. The following day I got up real early and went back into Houston. It was Tuesday, January 12, 1999. Things went much better this time. The Houston Chronicle interviewed me; I was covered by Channel 2 and two other channels that I was too busy to even bother with. People came and watched in large numbers and the police approached and then said I was doing nothing wrong. It was then that I found that my removal from Lafayette was aired nationally on "Inside Edition" and that they had heard I was coming. I left Houston for Austin and got the news there, again, Channel 2. I then drove all the damn way to San Antonio where the police told me to leave the city or go to jail. I then drove all the way to just outside of El Paso through countless hours of warm desert. When I got to my hotel room I called Mindy. We talked with excitement about national coverage and about her coming out to California. She said that I was her inspiration and at that point I again remembered why I do what I do and how I know I'm the man I say I am.

On Wednesday I got the news in El Paso, then I drove to the outskirts of Phoenix. There I worked out for several hours with some guy named Javier who owned the Toltec Inn and had a workout facility in one of the rooms. I gave him a copy of "Unlimited Development"- a fitness plan that I wrote several years back-because he seemed committed enough to want to look like me. He said he'd give me free hotel rooms here and there and whatever. I really needed to hit the weights and just thought it was miraculous that I came across some, wherever the hell I was. The Capital Building seemed a good spot to appear in Phoenix. I got the news and was then ushered over to San Diego. Crowds of store owners opening up told me that street performers were strictly prohibited as I strolled, as the Naked Cowboy, down the streets. It was nice out and I got on the news. I told those I passed after my news interview, "sorry about the no street performers thing." I got to Kenneth Beck's place in Hollywood that night and slept like a baby after reading "Unlimited Power" for two hours . Friday was my last day alone as the Naked Cowboy before Mindy would be with me for a week. I did Pasadena and got no press. I did however, get photos taken with the Sergeant, and several officers. They loved it and told me to come back later at night on the weekend when the place was hopping. I went back to Hollywood where I covered all of Hollywood Boulevard several times. The police let me pass when I gave them a "Naked Cowboy Tour Guide." He said as he let me go, "I just had to make sure you weren't a weirdo." Wow, what does it take here? When Mindy arrived that evening, we first went and unpacked her stuff at Ken's, then we went to Pasadena to storm through some big crowds on Colorado Boulevard. We were almost killed there by some serious punks. They followed close behind me screaming "faggot" and shit like that. We ate and went back to Hollywood. The week in California with Mindy was like a little paradise. We shared every waking moment of it together though we did do some work. Outside of performing on Venice Beach and getting on the news in Hollywood and Santa Barbara, and getting in the Los Angeles Times, we watched movies, ate, worked-out, everything. We stayed at the Blue Sands Hotel in Santa Barbara and had a pretend honeymoon together. We laid on the beaches along the Pacific Coast Highway and shared many loving moments together. My hit song "Sex on the Beach in Santa Barbara" was written during our time together. The day I took her back to the airport was a long goodbye. We did goal-setting exercises at the airport for a couple of hours before I left her there to catch her plane. The weekend after Mindy's departure was spent with Ken. He went with me to Venice Beach and the Boardwalk while I performed each day. We ate out together , watched movies and just pretty much bull-shitted about the entertainment business and what he knew of his end. I got him working out with me in the mornings, something he'd not been doing, and we hit if off like brothers. It was a productive and enjoyable mix of working and learning about life.

Monday began the real workweek and so after coffee with Ken, I was off for Las Vegas. I drove across a real hot strip of sand and arrived around noon. I wasn't in Las Vegas for more than fifteen minutes. I parked in front of the Stardust, called the news, got on the news and lots of photos with "Naked Cowboy" cheering tourists and then was quickly ushered to my car. "Hey, I'm getting good at this." I then drove back to Mesa Street in El Paso and got the same news coverage I had on the way to California before stopping outside of Houston for a second appearance there. The following morning I did Houston again with no coverage, but, with swarms of people, who had seen me on the news only a week or so ago, surrounding me. I gave out two hundred Naked Cowboy C.D.s that had finally been delivered to Ken's house in California just before leaving. I should have had this Naked Cowboy C.D. before leaving Cincinnati in the first place, but, I kept getting excuses from the replication group in New York. People tried to give me money, and some did. I think I got like ninety dollars which a number of high school girls collected for me by saying "donations?" They came out of nowhere and wanted to help me out. It was Tuesday. I had got a call from the Jenny Jones Show letting me know that my second appearance would air that day. "I love national exposure like you just can't believe." I was then thrown out of Texas prior to driving eight hundred and ninety miles. I hit another motel and called Mindy before falling asleep exhausted. I did run however, I'm not a lazy ass. The rest of the trip was pretty much rained out. I went to Little Rock, Arkansas, Memphis and lastly Nashville.

I did however stop back at Fridays on Eliston Place in Nashville to pass out the new CD to some old pals who seemed happy to see me. I then bolted home. It was Thursday, January 28, 1999 when I pulled back into Dewitt Street in Cincinnati. I immediately took a shower, and went to Mindy's and went to bed. The next morning I started thinking about Washington D.C. I just felt that I should have somehow included it in the tour and was feeling like I came home early. I wanted to send a package with my C.D. in it to Bill Clinton after hearing a radio evangelist blast on him and his administration on the way home through Little Rock. I then started thinking of publicity and got this idea to send the C.D. in a suspicious looking package with a note reading, isn't it time you heard the new Naked Cowboy C.D.? Luckily I consulted a friend who told me that nobody would think that was funny and that I would spend lots of time behind bars with no coverage. So I drove to Washington to take Bill a C.D. in person on January 31, 1999. I quickly found out the following day that you couldn't just go up to the White House steps as I had thought and so I went for a drive around Washington to find somewhere better. I made a turn down Connecticut and passed by two hundred or more TV cameras all facing the front door of the Mayflower Hotel. It was media madness as every news team across the United States was there to get a shot of Monica Lewinsky coming out of the hotel. She was there to testify about her relationship with the President. I couldn't believe it. I parked and ran over to the McDonalds that was next door, went into the bathroom and changed. I gave my clothes to the cashier saying, "I might be back for these, I might not." I then left and walked right in front of the Mayflower's entrance where I began to dance and sing, "I'm the Naked Cowboy coming to a town near you." I got Associated Press across the United States and front pages of newspapers everywhere as well. I got news coverage worldwide on both local channels and CNN. My photo on the front page of one paper was held up on "Regis and Kathy Lee" the following morning by which time I was at home in Cincinnati sleeping. Now I felt that the trip had come to successful end.

Chapter 6
Untitled

It wasn't more than a day after being home that I began feeling like a loser that needed to go out and do something with my life. Thankfully I had gotten a call from the Rick and Bubba Show in Birmingham Alabama. That got me out on the road again. Nashville was on the way so I stopped there. I got thrown out of town as usual and got on the news again. I spoke to Mindy when I got to Birmingham, and due to some sort of lover's quarrel we got into prior to leaving, it hurt even more than usual to be away from her. The Rick and Bubba Show went great. They'd heard of me while I was touring the country. They also happened to be the judges who gonged me at the Jenny Jones talent show. I was well covered by the media in Birmingham and also in Atlanta on the way home. I was passing through when I heard that Bill Clinton would be in Atlanta for Hank Aaron's birthday party. I staked out the hotel and appeared out front for cameras when I thought Bill's limousine had arrived. I got back to Cincinnati and then left immediately for Washington D.C. to play on the Capital Building steps. Turned out to be no big deal and no one gave a shit. I began to realize that the best success I'd had since the beginning of all this hoopla came from going where the media already happened to be, so I began to sit back and observe what was going on in the world. Why go out and continue to make something out of something that had already been covered and done. Just before this plan happened though, I took a trip to NYC with five friends from Fridays in a limo to try and get on the David Letterman Show again. No such luck. Back to my better idea, I began locally and then nationally. Beginning in my hometown I began to appear at every news covered event I could find. I did all of the festivals, parades and outdoor parties that occurred from February through May of 1999. I was banned from Tri-county mall; Cinergy Field, Showcase Cinemas; the University of Cincinnati's Campus, Newport Aquarium, Ault Park and the Cincinnati Courthouse just to name a few. I was thrown out of the Indianapolis 500, the Chicago MTV V.J. Contest, and was arrested and jailed for grand marshaling the Kentucky Derby Parade, unexpectedly. My friend Jim Knippenburg, with the Cincinnati Enquirer, covered a lot of the details following me in the paper, and local and syndicated radio shows accepted me every time I came to their stations which was fairly frequently. I worked at Fridays part-time throughout the entire period between February and May picking up shifts when I wanted to. They were very flexible that way for me which is why I continue to work there despite offers to work similar jobs in the local area offering more money for my novelty. Mindy moved into my apartment at the beginning of May, I think it was the ninth or so, and then her parents pulled up in a U-haul, moving her out on the sixteenth of the same month. She claimed I was dangerous and that I didn't want her there. I only recall working on my career and

53

wondering what the U-haul was doing in the front yard. The fact that we'd not talked for two days, to me, was not anything out of the usual. I didn't think so at the time anyway. In retrospect I know that I'd become the possessed maniac I often become when I loose sight of the river, jumping rock to rock up stream, with my raft in hand. I finished my third C.D. titled "Naked Cowboy, again" on the seventeenth and decided that I wanted to do another tour. This one, I decided had to include Mindy.

Chapter 7
Round Two

On June 11, 1999 I left home, this time with Mindy, for another trip across the United States. She had been talking for some time about finding a job with travel and I wanted to give her one. One without a paycheck, initially. We went straight to Nashville and I was in a police car with news coverage within fifteen minutes of parking. I was driven back to my car where Mindy had ended up as well.

Birmingham was our night out at the Quality Inn that was being provided by the Rick and Bubba Show. I was singing the National Anthem at a Rick and Bubba softball game the following night. When I got up to sing and they had me stroll down the ball field to home plate where all the players were lined up in two rows with their hands on their hearts, nobody could keep from bursting out in laughter.

Mindy and I then drove to Nashville again where we bought Fan Fair tickets from a scalper for the following day. We went in normal, in clothes, then I went up to the center stage as the Naked Cowboy and danced around till the police hauled me off. I took probably fifty photos with people before the police could even get to the crowd surrounding me.

We did Atlanta the following morning and spent the afternoon getting the engine put back in my car after it fell out at a stop sign in the ghetto. Several hours, and four hundred dollars later, we left Atlanta for Birmingham again. Mindy took a nap and I drove four hundred miles east to Birmingham. Yep, I went east, the wrong way. Mindy took over the driving at that point while I wrote in my journal. (Journal Entry) My current goal is to create the Naked Cowboy as a multi-billion dollar industry, merchandising comics, music, photos, clothing, and anything and everything else imaginable that can bear the Naked Cowboy's likeness and meaning, "determination." I want to feel satisfied with each day's efforts because I feel deep in my heart and soul that I did more than any other entertainer alive did! I'm going to know that I went the distance and made the difference.

I want to feel my unequaled level of determination in everything that I do. I want to be more ripped, built and disciplined than anyone. I want to feel, be and create these things because I know that God made me to do it. I want to be a communicator. I want to withstand my particular fight. To continually know and feel and cherish my unquestioned commitment to be the most famous man to ever live, love and enjoy this reign on Earth. I want to constantly hear the constant flood of compliments and the history of how the Naked Cowboy rose, rises and will continually stride towards being the most celebrated entertainer of all time. I want to be the most beautiful man alive. I want an image so strong that no one can deny me on sight. I want to appear as a star at all times. An absolute, unquestioned super star at all times. I want to be looked upon as the man that was unstoppable. The man that was determined to go the distance like no other. I want to look this way because God made me to look just this way. I want everyone alive to know that the Naked Cowboy is a loving man who had given them the finest model of the "Ultimate Success Formula" ever purposely created. I want my example and position as a role model to positively influence Humanity. Finishing my writing I looked up to see that Atlanta signs were beginning to appear again. Mindy had backtracked us to where I screwed up and went the wrong way. Leaving the highway in Atlanta for gas the car again broke down on the exit ramp. We pushed the car to a garage, walked to a hotel that was way out of the budget, and I thought to myself the whole damn way-" How am I supposed to believe all that shit I just wrote down when this happens?" Over the next three days we appeared in Birmingham, Baton Rouge, Lafayette, Louisiana, and Houston. We got multiple news coverage in each city. I was handcuffed only once, and released to play freely in every city. It was like, O.K. now to be out in public in your underwear playing guitar and calling yourself the Naked Cowboy. Still, we were approaching our fifth day of driving over ten hours a day and so we were getting a bit restless. Hotel-to-hotel living requires a great deal of discipline, especially if you are running, and doing push-ups, sit-ups, back-pulls and free-squats both morning and night. It was ironic, on Friday afternoon we decided to take some time off for ourselves. We stopped along a very hot, desert road at a wild life preserve. It was outside the desert somehow. Very green, with lakes and ponds. A picture perfect place to work on suntans after a long week's work. We found a secluded deck over a peaceful blue lake at the end of a very long and winding dirt road without seeing a soul. We put on our swimsuits and lay in the sun. Five minutes later a park ranger told us we had to leave because the preserve was not open to the public. We got back in the car and I drove another four hundred miles. Our entire weekend was spent in the one hundred degrees, plus, desert. We had a lot of road to cover through El Paso, Benson, Tucson, Phoenix, Needles and lastly Las Vegas.

Vegas was the "kick off the week with a good one," city. I played for just under three hours straight in the windiest bull shit weather imaginable. No news coverage, but thousands of photos taken away by tourists to every corner of the world. I called Charles Worthington, a friend in California, on cell phone, who navigated us to his place in Hollywood. We stayed at Charles' place, worked out in an actual workout facility and sat in a Jacuzzi for several hours. It was an awesome time of recovery and peace though it only lasted for about fourteen hours, including sleep. Hell yeah, we were up the following morning and on the Pacific Coast Highway by seven a.m. We drove to the outskirts of San Francisco and even stopped several times along the way to eat, and play on the beaches. The water was cold but bearable, and Mindy and I were becoming closer than ever as we fought to make a successfully moving, physically and mentally exhausting trip across the United States together without killing each other. We stayed at "-otel" that night. That's what a motel goes by when the first letter burns out. Wednesday, June 23, 1999 was the Naked Cowboy's first appearance on Market Street, or anywhere in San Francisco for that matter, ever, in his whole life. New experiences are just one of the many great benefits of my work. The city was like none I'd ever been in. Very pretty, clean, and hell, I don't know, it just looked cool. I didn't get any coverage but I did get a flowerpot thrown out of a window at me. Missed by a few inches. Would have killed me. Can't please everybody. Mindy wasn't feeling well and was making calls home to her doctor to get a prescription so I spent most of the time, roughly three hours, wandering the heavily peopled streets by myself.

The following day we got great news coverage in Reno, Nevada, and Friday we got four news channels in Salt Lake City. I had done phone interviews with the Gary Burbank Show, Rick and Bubba in Birmingham, and several others, all of which told me that Salt Lake City would be a bust because of it's strong religious affiliations. Just the opposite was true. They loved it, and ate it up like no other city to date. I never even saw a police officer despite the fact that Mindy and I, between my climbing up on landscaping and singing, and her passing out hundreds of Naked Cowboy fliers, caused non-stop commotion for over two hours.

Mindy and I had exciting plans for the weekend. My good friend Bill, who lives back in Cincinnati, had a meeting scheduled at the Beaver Creek Resort in Colorado for the weekend. Well, Mindy and I made it a point to be there as well. Ten dollars got our car parked, and we stayed with Bill at the Embassy Suites. Swimming, feeding horses, lying out in the hot sun, eating out, and whirl pools were the agenda for the duration of the weekend. Oh, and of course, working out like a tri-athlete in the hotel's weight room. Roughly seven thousand miles behind us, it was a nice break from the action. In fact, being with Mindy anywhere, after the workday is done, is like a honeymoon. The last three days of our journey was not much different from the majority of the first seventeen. We drove city to city trying to get on the news by simply showing up in the middle of each visited city as the Naked Cowboy and causing a stir. Mindy and I were both homesick now and our fuses were short. I wanted a fabulous outburst of enthusiasm when she made her calls to the various cities' news desks, and I think she just wasn't into it any more. Really though, I felt like I should have been doing it all along and was kicking myself for entrusting any part of anything to anybody. See what I mean, the fuses were getting short. We were completely ignored in Denver, got the news in Kansas

City, and got news all over the country with the appearance on Monument Square in Indianapolis. We pulled into Cincinnati on Wednesday, twenty days after leaving home in the first place. I dropped Mindy off at her mother's house and went to perform at the Q102 Party in the Park at Cincinnati's Sawyer Point. I just wasn't tired yet. That night, and the following, we rested and lived as the closest couple in the world, ironically, as we are destined to be.

On July 3, 1999, we left again for Washington D.C. A quick ten hour drive to grand marshal the Nations July 4th Parade. Of course no one knew we were coming but us, but what difference does that make? What's seven hundred miles when you just drove over eight thousand. It was well over one hundred degrees, this time with humidity. Did I mention my 1984, BMW, 318I doesn't have air-conditioning. It was hot as holy shit.

On the Fourth, we stood in front of the National Archives building where the parade was to begin at 11:00 a.m. and we both were just drenched with sweat. Speeches were being made in respect to our nation and the celebrated parade that was about to begin as I disrobed. "Mr Moody and ladies and gentlemen," the announcer spoke. Mindy looked at me as I stood a foot above the crowd and said, "is he talking to you?" When the parade began, I strolled out in front of it, singing and dancing as I do. No one batted an eye outside of what you'd expect to see at a parade. Two-hundred yards later I was met by two policemen that eased their way to the center with me and led me to one side where the crowds were gathered. They told me to stay away. I went down through the crowds a few blocks and then returned to the front of the parade. I was led out three times before passing the booth where a female narrator of sorts, reported live, what was happening in the parade for a televised audience. When I passed she said, "and here we have, „ the Naked Cowboy. Some people know how to keep cool." This still seemed like total bullshit cause it was over one-hundred degrees and I was sweating profusely. Once passed this point, Mindy and I went back to the car and returned to Cincinnati. It was a very, very long drive under the conditions of a heat advisory. The second tour was over. What next, was not yet defined, but developing? I was glad to have closure and anxious to see what might develop as a result of so much action taken.

Chapter 8
The Way I Am

Over the next month or so, I just stayed local. I worked almost every night at Fridays, and Mindy was still living at her mother's, maybe her friends. I went to all of the main events that occurred in Cincinnati, St. Rita's Festival, the WEBN fireworks, Seafood Festival, Jazz Festival, Shutzenfest. I'm telling you, if there was more than a thousand people there, there was also a guy playing guitar in his underwear while singing through the crowds. My financial situation had grown to just over three thousand dollars debt, now, on two different credit cards, which was, of course, why I was working as many shifts as I could pick up, careful not to interfere with my Naked Cowboy schedule. I was vowing not to leave town on anything speculative without the money to pay for it so I was beginning to feel constrained, but in that situation, I began to work harder and harder to create some new options. It may also be that when I work like a crazed maniac, I get to look so ripped and determined, I just feel unstoppable to the point of having no worries. Working harder has always tended to monopolize my time since for me working harder means from before sun-up, till way, way after sundown. I take no amenities, no laxity in diet or exercise regimen and no down time. Down time is any time where I'm not doing something directly related to being a one hundred percent bad ass, even if that means just being out in public with a cool outfit on and reinforcing my sense of confidence. I forget often times that there is a whole other layer of life outside the realm of eating, breathing, drinking and working perfection. You know, like a family that surrounds me with the only constraints of a few minutes, or a loved one only in the next room. I often times confuse being perfect (hardest working) with being selfish. I think I'm working around the clock solely for the sake of creating amazing feats of creativity and focus, but then suddenly I realize that I am out of focus and simply pushing everything imaginable that means anything out while I hide behind feelings of inadequacy. I persist and work with levels of determination that are simply unimaginable in order to legitimatize my worth. I literally reinvent myself when I get tired of beating up the guy I can be for sometimes less than a week. Mindy sometimes retreats, and I let her cause deep down I know she understands that I am always trying to improve, and it's just something people need to evaluate for themselves at times in order to really make progress. My love for her doesn't decline when I'm respecting my inner reclusive child. It's just scared of the security that she represents for me.

Chapter 9
You're Invited

Mindy had her pillows all fluffed up and positioned under her just so before our drive began for Minneapolis. I drove for eleven hours and it was pleasant. We stayed in Kenosha, Wisconsin at a Knights Inn that was paid for by the Dark Star radio program. We both had crusted sea bass and a romantic evening in a very nice, clean environment with movies. It was arranged the way it should be for a star. I go into the hotel, a fine hotel, say my name at the reception desk and I'm instantly helped and escorted to my room. The whole experience is really humbling. They don't know that I'm really still at the bottom. They just know that I'm here with the local radio program, I'm all paid, whatever I want, and I look and sound important. Frankly, I really don't need all the attention. The following morning, we went across the street to the radio station. You see everything is easy when you're invited. The personnel were very nice and so we waited and talked before taking a shuttle bus to the Minnesota State Fair. We were ushered into a booth from the rear where the program was broadcast live and Dark Star introduced me. I went out, talked with him for a minute about what I thought I was doing with my life then he had me sing a song. I stood before a crowd of fifty to one hundred people who upon completion of a full song, singing, and really moving, just stared without making a sound. I let the crowd know that it was all right. They could clap if they wanted. I talked with Dark again and they laughed at everything I said, as I was being completely serious. I sang two more songs, as the crowd remained completely silent. They weren't being hateful; they just didn't seem to know what to think. I said it then and I'll say it now, if Elvis Presley were there doing the same exact thing, having never done what he'd already done, he'd have gotten the same response. My outfit is astonishing, my deliverance is very energetic, I sound presentable, but I'm not like anything you've ever seen before. Mindy and I left immediately after my part on the program and we drove to Chicago.

I simply will not go that far away from home without stopping for any and all good publicity attempts. We parked in a public garage, called the media repeatedly, and I sang and danced on the busiest street we could find in Chicago. Twenty minutes later I was picked up by the Chicago Police Paddy Wagon and carted to the police station. When I got there Mindy was right behind me. She forced the officer to bring her along also because I hadn't given her the car key yet and she would have been stranded without knowing what was going on. I signed autographs at the Chicago Police Station for about an hour as a citation was written. The chief came in laughing and holding up a pair of underwear and asking Mindy if she'd like to try them on. It was a big joke to them, they even apologized and let Mindy and I go back to the car in the paddy wagon. I was told by two officers that the ticket was just a formality, and to ignore the appearance in court. "This will get lost in administration. You don't need to worry about it," is exactly what the officers told me. Meanwhile Mindy was all excited about getting to drive in the paddy wagon as she exclaimed, "hey I've never been in one of these." I told her, "hey, stick with me, you'll go places."

The next place she went was Birmingham, Alabama for the Rick and Bubba Fat Fest. It was September 10, 1999 when she boarded my car for this one. I again drove some eleven hours again before we reached the Quality Inn in Birmingham. We ate good and slept in another king sized, very comfortable bed, with movies. All expenses paid and a televised event to occur for the Naked Cowboy the following day. What more could one ask for in my underwear. It was an arena, outdoors, that held over five thousand. It would be the biggest crowd I'd ever played for, as a scheduled artist and I was excited to be a part of it. We arrived at the amphitheater early the following day. It was warm outside in Birmingham and we checked out the scene. A big stage, a huge arena, lots of equipment for the scheduled performers. Scheduled were: Casio Kid, a comedian; Three on a String; someone named Derryberry, a local favorite who performed as a "Christian" singer; Mr. Lucky; and the Rick and Bubba Band. I was the second act and decided I'd better come up with some dialogue. I had my own changing/green room where I rehearsed some lines with Mindy as my audience. I stopped over to the green room where Rick and Bubba and everyone else performing or even preparing for the event was hiding out. The two green rooms were caddy corners to each other. They were all happy to see me and showed me off to those who'd not seen me before.

Mindy didn't want to leave the room she was in so we sat in our own room by ourselves. I performed and said the lines I'd came up with only minutes before going on stage and the crowd seemed happy. They clapped and cheered at the end of my songs, and laughed at my dialogue. I had an interview with a cameraman for the event, and then I stood in a pair of shorts and boots and sold CDs to people who were interested. I was at the same table with the "Christian" singer and so I was seen as the devil by many who dropped off "get saved" materials to help me come back to Christ. The people putting on the event had booths specifically for this. I sold twenty-eight CDs and the people in charge wouldn't even take their commission because they felt sorry for me. They couldn't understand what I was so happy about. I told them look, I'm used to showing up uninvited, getting kicked out and having my CDs thrown at me. Today I was supposed to be here, the crowd didn't kill me or throw things at me, and I sold twenty eight CDs- more than I've ever sold in my life. Things are looking up, believe it or not!

On our way back to Cincinnati I heard an advertisement on the radio for the Smyrna Air Show in Nashville. We waited in a long line of cars and parked for something shitty like twenty bucks. We then walked for a blooming country mile and a half and got situated in a huge crowd . Security was everywhere because it was at an air force base. Mindy and I met outside the Port-o-Let where she handed me the guitar bag. I went in, then came out giving her the guitar bag that was now containing my clothes. I strolled around for about fifteen minutes before being escorted out of the area by police officers and security personnel. I drove us back home to the village of Greenhills arriving some five hours later. I dropped Mindy off at a phone at the local shopping mall while I went over to make a round through the crowd at the O.L.R. Oktoberfest on the Commons. It was a last ditch effort just for the local crowd. The local police instantly grabbed me, and took me to my car. Mindy and I went to my apartment that was less than two minutes away. After running for thirty minutes and hitting the boxing bag, I was tired enough to go to sleep, and happy again to be with Mindy at our place.

Chapter 10
References

It was simply an offer too great to be refused. I'd only been home for about, hell, I don't know, it was now September 22, 1999. It was a call from a guy in Nashville to whom I'd sent my first C.D. "Small Town Crusader," with me as John Robert Burck. I had originally heard of him through an old, reputable modeling contact in New York City, Mike Lyons. I also sent him my first Naked Cowboy C.D. with all the press I'd collected to date. He was calling to tell me that he'd been trying to tie up some financial ends for quite some time and that now he was ready to give me the opportunity of a lifetime.

I left for Nashville, knowing that much two days later. Airfare was paid and set up and I was to shoot photos to be used for promotional material to represent John Robert Burck, the model and actor. He picked me up at the airport and then took me to a hotel in the middle of Nashville. It was the Loews and the top floor, which occupied the entire top of the hotel. He made it a point to tell me that the room cost over one thousand dollars a night. We then went to eat and he came across as a deadly serious, businessman with a plan. He told me of all of his past successes involving both movie development and music industry work. He said that the particular line of business he was currently engaged in, the telecommunications industry, made him uniquely prepared to launch the most incredible entertainment career for the right person. He couldn't tell me enough times that I was ten times more than he'd expected and that I simply blew away his expectations. He said, " you will undoubtedly be the new standard for supermodels in the new millennium. That we would be able to then segue that into motion pictures and do whatever we wanted." We got back to the hotel around midnight and we were both extremely excited and enthusiastic about shooting some incredible promotional material. He spent an hour or so, unpacking equipment from his car and setting up a make shift photography studio in our hotel's living room. It was 4:00 A.M. before we began shooting. We shot over thirty rolls of film. He had outfits from several top name designers, and I wore them all in every different pose, position, expression available for my face and body. We did these sweaty, steamy waist up shots in the whirlpool for an hour as well and that left me feeling faint as I drifted off to sleep on the couch sitting up.

The next morning I was served breakfast, and I went down to workout in the hotel's workout facility. When I got back we talked and he told me all kinds of crazy cool shit. He told me that I wasn't to work any more. In fact, that nothing was too expensive, nothing was too good for me. He said as for his representing me, that I was now to be treated so well that anybody else's treatment of me would be "unconscionable." He said that he would give me money to go home with and that I needed to set up a bank account in my hometown so that he could keep it full for anything that I needed. We shot photos for the four hours before heading back to the airport. While waiting to leave for Cincinnati, he and I waited together and chatted. When it was time to leave he shook my hand and said that we were going to "rock the world."

When I got back to Cincinnati, Mindy and I were able to spend a lot more time together because I stayed out of Fridays to concentrate on my songs and my physique. Believing that things were going to turn around in a major way I relaxed and centered on the things that would make me king. Everyone who was close to me was excited and expecting great things from me. Everyone said, "we knew your time would come, congratulations, and, I knew it." I spoke with my new friend in Nashville every day. He told me the photography was out of this world, and that all the promotional engines were rolling. He also began to say some shit that I didn't really want to hear. Things like, "Well, when you left on the plane, back to Cincinnati, you didn't seem at all hurt to go." "I feel like you like what I can give you, but not me personally." We got into screaming fights over the following week over what this relationship was all about. I was straight forward from the beginning and never once deluded him. Somehow we always wound up not disagreeing, but he was definitely trying to see where my comfort zones were in regards to my sexuality and his future role in marketing it. He told me of his previous client a hundred times and how he had let him down, never really telling me the details. He played like he was just trying to see how much this whole idea of being the "most celebrated entertainer of all time" really meant to me. Since it meant everything, I passionately told him so in a way that would melt the stars from the sky. At one point during the first week he had me run down to an affiliate of AFTRA located in Cincinnati. I did paperwork and got registered with the union. I would become a professional actor, so I had to be a member. He was going to send the check for seven hundred and fifty bucks to have me enrolled. It was one of the first steps to getting me going. Then he sent me some professionally made headshots and composites with the photography he'd shot. It was all as professional as I'd seen. I was very excited and couldn't hide it if I'd tried. Mindy on the other hand, wasn't talking much about it. She was staying at her mom's more often now and I pretended I just didn't care because again I felt that my success was being looked down upon as a result of her worries. I didn't want to admit that things were looking too good to be true and I hated to admit that my angel wanted to protect me who was still at times being shielded by an iron shield of ego. "Like I couldn't be counted on to decipher between good and bad or otherwise threatening?" Her position became much harder to ignore however, when this nutcase in Nashville began telling me that he'd need to know when and where I was having sex, as I was his most valuable asset in the world. The final bomb came when he just bluntly said, "I'll have to be aware of every orgasm you have and they will have to be with me." Well, the Naked Cowboy came out of the closet at that point. No I didn't become gay. I took out my boots, hat, guitar, and undies out of the closet to practice in the mirror.

As for my friend in Nashville, he was told, "you know, I'm really not interested anymore." I followed up with, "Naked Cowboy forever!" I called everyone I'd spoken with and told them "false alarm," but stayed out of Fridays. Mindy was very happy, but was kind, cause she was certain I was let down. She didn't say I told you so, she didn't bat an eye, just stood there confident in my corner looking to protect my heart from the next intruder while leaving hers open to endure my selfish pride. Many close friends told me to kill my new "business partner," but I really wasn't that upset after about an hour and a half. What I gained in confidence from the security of another act of compassion under the wing of my love's umbrella made the downside trivial. Besides, the Naked Cowboy, I remembered, began as a result of several occurrences like this one. It was my way of setting up on my own terms. I didn't have to be discovered, or hired, or hand picked. I just had to do my own thing and create my own space in this whole big picture of life. I was very certain of it before this, and nothing really happened to make me think otherwise. By being the world famous Naked Cowboy, people are going to come to me with offers from every corner of the world. This first one was a bad deal, so I put it aside and began to look for ways to drum up more offers. It's that simple.

Height: 6' 2"
Hair: Black
Eyes: Hazel
Waist: 31
Suit: 42L
Shirt: 16 x 34
Inseam: 34
Shoe: 11

Rick Day

Color by Devron Tech. USA (212) 545-9380

Chapter 11
East Coast Tour

"I'm sorry, but what you're doing is cool as shit," is
what Steve Hampton said to me as I was leaving
Parrillo Performance. We had just packed the car with
Parrillo Bars and other Parrillo products. They had
issued me a check for fourteen hundred dollars and I
was on my way around the eastern end of the United
States. Parrillo was the first one to give me money to
do my thing and I vowed to be eternally grateful. His
products and advice have definitely been the
foundation that built the physique of the Naked
Cowboy. Steve was the manager there, and like
everyone else who knew me, thought packing up all
of my belongings and traveling on my own in my
underwear was cool.

The first city I hit after leaving Cincinnati was
Columbus. I decided that going across the United
States, as I had in the past, westward, was crazy.
National media attention can come from anywhere,
and going east gave me the opportunity to hit more
places, without driving ten hours, day after day, to get
to them. National news puts me in every state.
Columbus was fabulous. I called the media as in the
past and went to High Street. No more than ten
minutes had passed and I was passing out Parrillo
fliers and Parrillo Bars for three news channels. I did
interviews with each one and then moved on.
Cleveland was my next stop. I was there for the

dinner rush and was ignored. I've found that the news isn't very receptive, at least not to me, after the lunch and mid-day rush. I was taken to my car by hoards of police officers while being laughed at by hundreds of onlookers.

The following day I hit Buffalo, New York. I played up and down a busy street next to a hot dog vendor where loads of people came out in support. I got the Associated Press, which landed me in newspapers across the United States and even in my hometown of Cincinnati. I then drove to Rochester and got on News Channel Ten. Wednesday came and I was in Albany, New York. I had a map I was following with all the cities I wanted to hit on it circled, but for no reason in particular. In Albany I played on the steps of several buildings that surrounded a huge public park. I had no police interference that I wasn't able to dispel. On each building's steps where I performed, word spread quickly and the people poured out. I gave out hundreds of fliers, all Parrillo, to very eager people. One lady said she had just talked to Steve Hampton at Parrillo's and said that he was trying to reach me. She had called Parrillo already to order Parrillo Bars as a result of a flier she'd just gotten. When I called Steve he said he got calls from every city I'd been in for the last three days and that I was "kicking ass."

I hit Springfield, Massachusetts that afternoon and got a live interview with Kix radio and did a local newspaper interview. I again had no police interference and made a medium size splash. Did I mention that throughout this whole tour so far, it was cold? On Thursday, it was thirty degrees when I hit Copley Square in Boston. I played three, one-hour performances for thousands of onlookers and that's all. Each news station I'd talked to sounded very interested and that kept me alive above and beyond the general public's response, which is always very powerful for me.

I thawed out over a period of hours driving, but at the time, I wasn't cold. I ducked in a coffee shop after each set to get my natural skin color back. That night I got a page from a guy in Hackettstown, New Jersey who dubbed himself a personal manager. He came across my website while surfing the internet. He said he had a lot of contacts in New York and asked if I'd be willing to go to a casting call for the Guiding Light. I was in a hotel room, at the time he asked. I was several hundred miles from home living on a credit card again by this time, as Parrillo money was long gone. By this time it seemed as if I was trying to make anything at all happen . I said, "of course I would." He asked me if I'd go in clothes to the casting call. Quickly aware of his lack of intelligence I said, "no, I'd be going in underwear and taking my friend Lou Ferrigno who would be wearing a suit, tie, and green makeup." We made plans to talk again after I made it clear that I'd just had a short, bullshit experience with another fool trying to call himself a personal manager and that he'd be wasting his time if he couldn't recognize legitimacy when it hit him in the face. I called Mindy as I'd been doing nightly and then went to sleep. The Big Apple was the next stop. It was cold as all hell, but invigorating. Hundreds of thousands of people were there as usual. I got Associated Press again and at least three news channels. I parked in my usual spot and gave everybody who worked there Parrillo Bars hoping to get my car back in one piece. I played for several hours and got out of the city immediately following my act. I stayed at the Roxbury Circle Motel just outside of Hackettstown as the new personal manager guy was supposed to call me the following morning. I ran and I worked out with my weights that I was lugging back and forth from my car to the hotel room each night as I moved day to day. I did New York City again on Saturday and again got an incredible response from the people. It's all tourists there, like the Boardwalk in Venice. I had thousands of photos taken, I bet, every ten minutes. Photos that would be going all over the world to be developed and talked about. I love that. I also loved calling Mom, Dad, and others and saying, "oh, I'm just hanging out on Times Square getting ready to play." When I was ready to leave, I'd not yet heard from the personal manager guy so I began heading towards Washington. Halfway between New York City and Washington, he called and said he'd been trying to call repeatedly. Oh yeah, pagers don't work at the bottom of parking garages in New York City. I rerouted and went to his house in Hackettstown. It was about five hours out of my way but the room would cost nothing and he could turn out to be someone who actually knew how to help.

When I arrived he was waiting outside. I went in, made myself at home, ate, and went to bed after he told me how incredible I was and how he expected he could make me a fortune because I was" a gold mine." I already knew these things and was quickly bored, but said I'd give him a shot. Sunday, Sunday night, Monday and Monday night were spent relaxing more or less at my new personal manager's house. We shot loads of photos to be used for promotional material. I went to one of his acting classes that he taught in Hackettstown and I sat and watched a couple of movies. It was all a nice rest before a long drive home.

Mindy felt a little uneasy about the situation knowing that I could very well be spending more time away to get a new partnership, off the ground. We had disagreements but knew in our hearts that no challenge would be to great for our love to conquer. We tried several times to find common ground but we were both scared and unable to resolve our differences that were really just meaningless insecurities on both of our parts as we tried to deal with the reality of a possibly long separation from each other. On Tuesday I drove to Washington D.C. I played for two hours and passed out six hundred Parrillo fliers. I got no news, but one newspaper. I was a bit disheartened, but thinking back, I got the news so big there before because I went to where the reporters were already stationed. This is Washington D.C., a very big and explosive place. It's the Nations Capitol, and I'm just a guy in my underwear. I drove back to Cincinnati the same day. I made a grand total of fourteen hours of driving to an empty apartment. I slept like a baby and can't remember dreaming that night.

Chapter 12
"Honey, I Miss You"

On Monday, October 18, 1999 I stopped by Parrillo Performance to have a quick photo shoot with John Parrillo before heading back to New Jersey. I shot many rolls of film and was happy with the work that was posted and complete before my eyes as a lot of the work was done on a digital camera. I was ripped and cool looking. I was making it out of town without ever even hearing Mindy's voice, which to me was almost crippling. After Parrillo's I drove for several hours not reaching Hackettstown until nearly midnight. Tuesday and Wednesday were spent making photos and workout videos to be sold at nakedcowboy.com. My personal manager friend spent his whole day and night, from what I saw, at the computer smoking cigarettes and drinking coffee while building an improved website that was only getting hits when I went out and did something.

Thursday, October 21, 1999 I drove into New York City for just such an occurrence. I appeared on the Today Show by showing up at Rockefeller Center in my underwear with a guitar. Then after leaving there, I went to a pay phone on Times Square and called information to get the address for the Howard Stern Show that was on in my car as I was leaving the city. I got it and went there in my underwear again. I went to the information booth in the main lobby and said, "I'm here for the Howard Stern Show." The guy said, "fourteenth floor." I went up, got on the Howard Stern Show and then drove back to Hackettstown where my personal manager friend says he's been getting calls from everywhere and hits on the website. Like I didn't know how this whole thing works. A week had passed and I was on my way back to Cincinnati again. I was to appear at a radio show sponsored event in Erie, Pennsylvania on Friday and it was halfway between home and Hackettstown, but not really. I'd broke down and paged Mindy who I desperately knew I needed in my life. I drove through Pittsburgh on my way home and got a couple of newspaper interviews by appearing in the City Square and passing out Parrillo fliers. I returned home around five in the evening and took Mindy to the Olive Garden where we eat every time we make up. It was awesome as was our time together that night and the next day. It was over too soon, however, as I was back on the road on Thursday again.

I left around noon, after three workouts, and drove till midnight again stopping at a hotel that ended up being only ten minutes from the radio show that I was to be on the following morning. I did appear and was interviewed around 7:00 a.m. Friday morning, then I appeared on the news playing guitar in my underwear in front of a bar called JR's in the afternoon. I was then displayed on the back of a trolley car that drove all over the city promoting the radio station. It was cold and crazy. Two drunk DJs and a mob of people who had won tickets to go on this ride. The trolley ride ended again at JR's where I hung around until late at night to appear on stage as an opening act for a headlining comedian. They got me a hotel that night and then I drove to Hackettstown the following day. Knowing what has worked in the past and what has not worked once, I decided to use Hackettstown as a place to stay where I could get in and out of New York City as cheaply as possible. The personal manager guy could try and drum up whatever he wanted as far as I was concerned, but as of yet he has come up empty every time. I went into the city and performed on Times Square the first Saturday and Sunday, and then five times over the following week.

Those appearances got me on MTV, Fox and Friends, several news channels, and several newspapers. Meanwhile, my personal manager guy worked like a soldier on my website and pushed and promoted with videos we made to everyone under the sun who'd already said no ten times. The guy couldn't get it through his head that I was not a star with some fascinating story to tell about a new C.D. or a movie, or a music video or anything like that. I was a complete nobody, with nothing to tell, and just a burning desire to be famous. I was more than willing to accept that I was looking desperate. It's the act. It's a guy who is willing to be famous for being at the bottom. A determined man with a humanitarian mission based on humility and perseverance. "Do I look like a star?" Well, I do, but not an ordinary one for sure. I'm going to be an American Icon. It takes lots of promotion and many closed doors. I remember being at Fox and Friends studio and they said they wanted me outside for the weather report. Well my personal manager was with me, thinking we'd have an indoor interview, professional-like, and he gets ready to blow up over the "outside" thing. I had to tell him to "shut the hell up and get over it." I'm getting ready to have a good, national plug and he's worrying about how we're being treated. This kind of shit began to piss me off and it ran through everything the guy did.

Mass work on web sites, video, film and professional stationary to showcase a guy who wanted to look desperate but entertaining. Think about it, I could get booked to play in a bar for fifty bucks and play for thirty, maybe forty people. I could do it nightly, be taken seriously, and in the long term, make a living at it. Who the hell wants that? Well ,not me? I'd rather play for free and look like an idiot for millions. It's the kind of thing an innovator does. It's the kind of action that a man would take to do it like no one else ever has. That's why it's magical, and I do it best, on top of all that. The worst thing of all, was that this guy is constantly telling me everything I don't want to hear. "You're looking great." "You're the only guy I've ever met who's willing to do so much for your own career." "You're a gold mine just waiting your turn," and shit like this. Now I don't want to sound like an asshole, but I know this crap and don't want to be flattered. Get me something I can't get myself or forget it. He's also telling me that I really need to be there, at his place, to really see all these things come to fruition. That "Mindy better get used to you being away" and bullshit like that. No way! I'm like thinking I'm the only one who's making things happen, and your time is quickly running out. His big plans to get me to see all of these connections of his were just other friends of his who happened to work for professional talent groups in New York. I was this guy's star the minute I walked in his door and he never tried to deny it. In fact, he happily professed it. His flashy-named connections in the acting and modeling business in New York had just gotten burned by the last string of less-than-really-determined clients that my dedicated personal manager guy had represented. This made them unwilling to see the real McCoy, me, before the holidays, which as far as I was concerned, was the deadline for the current living arrangement, at least. Sure, if he gets me something, I'll come out, but I am not waiting here in Hackettstown, hundreds of miles from the things I love, to start at the bottom of an acting career. I am not starting at the bottom.

That's how the Naked Cowboy came about. A guy who began outside of the normal way of doing things without needing to follow orders or guidelines. A guy who was completely willing to be himself, and not some butt-kisser who manipulated the people around him to shuffle his obvious talents to a bunch of preying pimps. I'm resting on virtues and quality efforts to make a difference and I'm sustained by sincerity. I don't want to be a guy who succeeded in the entertainment industry; I want to be a guy who succeeded in life through entertainment. That's not about money, or flashy titles, or hyped promotional rhetoric, it's about loving to entertain, and doing it lovingly while enriching all those I love.

I missed Mindy terribly and had to get back home to her. I was suffering as a human knowing that our love was so fantastic, and my selfish, pride-driven desires were keeping me from going about this "career thing" with my priorities in line. Again it was the, "I'm looking for the end result without considering the means" thing again. It is the "means" that determine the "ends."

I drove to Cincinnati on Monday, October 15, 1999 and met with my Mindy first thing. We were united in love and on the same page we'd always been on since the day I'd met her. Note: I sincerely apologize to my personal manager friend for sounding so unkind in my representation of his actions on my behalf. He worked day in and day out to serve my objectives. He cared and was a true friend to me outside of our professional attempts to work together.

My aggression, my fervor, and disapproval come from my own anger at myself for not sticking to my original plan of action. That plan was to market and promote myself until I became a star, and then, and only then, to seek representation to market me if I then decided to go that route. He is surely great, enthusiastic, and most effective at what he does. I was simply foolish and impatient. I wanted him to specialize in something other than what he was accustomed to specializing in. Then I was upset with him for not doing the most effective job. He wanted to be my friend and I treated him wrongly. I ignored his efforts at friendship, in order to pay attention to my big dreams. Again, still not awake to the most essential ingredients of a hero's welcome, honoring the traits that create a hero in the first place.

Chapter 13
Personal Journal Entry

Tuesday, November 16, 1999 "Inventory of Dreams"
I want to be the "most celebrated entertainer of all
time." I want to share my life's experience with
everyone who is alive now, and will live hereafter. I
want to share my unequaled level of persistence and
commitment with the world. I want to be the best
built, best-looking man, in the opinion of all,
including myself, alive. I want everyone who
witnesses me, and that shall include everyone,
through my image and actions, to know that I was
simply unstoppable. I want to be the dominant figure
of what the male body, mind and spirit is capable of
being. I want everything about me to communicate
complete and unquestioned perfection. I want to give
all that I have to actualize my absolute fullest
potential for all of mankind. I want to continue to
improve myself until even I am satisfied. I want all of
my relationships to be fruitful and prosperous. I want
everyone who comes in contact with me to depart
from me feeling compelled to improve themselves
even if all they do is pass without seeing me.
Physically, socially, emotionally and spiritually I want
complete solidarity with God. I want to create and
nurture a mind that is simply unconquerable. I fully
intend to use the entertainment and political arenas to
maximize my impact on humanity. Everything that I
do will radiate and accelerate my loving agenda.
Manners and kindness will be my trademarks.

Honesty will be my primary tool for success. My intentions are one hundred percent selfless and loving. My strategy is to spread my own unique magic everywhere I go. The riches of the world are mine for the asking. My relationships will continue to grow, my body, mind, spirit and level of unchallenged beauty will flourish, and God will reward me at every turn for my efforts. My goals will begin to actualize through the media throughout the world. I will begin to make my presence and stamina known to humanity by persevering and refusing to accept anything less than the world's center stage!

Chapter 14
Funny Stuff

Well it didn't take long to become a comedian. I did it in, oh, one day. It was Thanksgiving Day when I found this really cool pair of fake "Bubba" teeth in the Greenhills Tanning Salon. I'd been looking for something to make the comedy I'd been writing for month's sound funny. The kinds of experiences that I was having were easy to wrap comedy around, but in the end, if you didn't know who the Naked Cowboy was, you wouldn't get it. Mindy actually thought of the teeth idea. I just put together all kinds of goofy rhetoric about my experiences on and off the road as the Naked Cowboy as if I really looked like I did with the teeth in, all along. They made a perfect man look like a perfect man with huge, ugly, rotten, protruding teeth. Like every other idea I've had, I went nuts with it. I practiced in front of the mirror for hours each day. I sang comedic songs like, "Heeeeeee, I feel a little bit horse tonight," and "quit teething me." Everybody I performed for laughed hysterically as they told me why it wasn't "really" funny. I had one liners to cover the molar system and nobody could believe the profile I was creating. Comedy gave me a chance to step out from behind the guitar and just act stupid . Many good friends and business consultants said that my routine really had a good bite. I was committed to the idea of being a comedian however and so that was the product I'd be taking back to Hackettstown. Hell, after wearing the damn things the whole of

Thanksgiving Day that I spent with my family, my act was polished the first day. It was November 30, however, when I did leave for Hackettstown. I'd talked several times with my personal manager before leaving to tell him what was up. I'd sang him a parody or two on the phone and he was as excited as I was. Nobody didn't laugh, but all still professed, "I don't really know if it's funny."

In Hackettstown I practiced daily, for hours, not just performing with an invisible microphone in the mirror, but with singing my seventy-eight songs a day, and working out like an animal. I was incredibly ripped and hungry. We shot videos to highlight the comedy and re-submitted to everyone I'd ever sent to before as if for the first time.

A good friend of mine in Cincinnati told me that "I was only seven minutes away from a spot on the Letterman or the Tonight Show, with a comedy skit." I shot photos with the teeth and went into New York City each day for over a week harassing people and being insane on Times Square before countless thousands of people. "Hey, you know where I can find a good club or a bar? To beat you over the head with?" "Not just another pretty face ladies and gentleman." "Don't be intimidated by my beauty." "Who needs a body, when you've got a face like mine?" All day long, for days, I had everyone who passed me on Times Square laughing his or her ass off. I also made another appearance on the Howard

Stern show by simply showing up and being crazy. I got lots of practice and was extremely exhausted each day after performing for three to four hours, and driving three. The minute I'd get back to the personal manager's house each day, he'd be chasing me down the hall with all kinds of talk about all the work he'd been doing for me all day and how lucky I was to have him working for me. To me it was just hype because nothing was set up, no money was coming in, and I know I was the only one "really" working. I'm not bitching, I don't think there was anything he really could do. I just had to do what I was doing and really just needed a place to stay while I was doing it. I'd spelled that out to him several times. I also said several times that I didn't' care that that was all I thought he could do, but he would get upset saying I just thought of him as a "glorified secretary." I did think that, so damn what. It's about getting the job done, not about titles or hype. Bottom line, he was a guy who probably could manage a star, but who couldn't. "Hey, I've got Brad Pitt here, I'd like to have him at your event." Who the hell wouldn't take a deal like that? Stars' names are worth their weight in gold. He couldn't get it through his head we weren't handling a star yet, we were creating a star. I know how to do that and am doing it this minute. He's no star and never made one, therefore he had no place debating me at any time concerning my strategy. Worst of all, he played way too heavy on the "friendship" card. He was my manager to me, nothing else. I don't mix business and pleasure when it comes to the essential decisions for my life's work. His dialogue bored me and irritated me till the last straw was burned. I had to see results. I had to see how his expertise could further me and it was strictly what I was doing that was creating the results.

He did call Parrillo Performance after I'd gotten them loads of local and national news to negotiate a monthly salary for representing their products. Parrillo Performance loved me though, and again, I'd have made that call myself with the same or better responses, being as I was the one who passed out Parrillo Bars all over the eastern United States in my underwear causing the phones to ring off the hook at Parrillos home office in Cincinnati. All it did to have someone else speaking for me was to insure that I didn't "really" know what was going on. Another sponsor, Vision Fit International, called to invite me to sing at the "Jingle Ball" in Pittsburgh on December 13, 1999. I played and sang as the Naked Cowboy at a black tie event sponsored by a radio show, B-94, the Mix. Vision Fit had contacted me through Parrillo Performance and it was again, about half way between Hackettstown and home. There was no doubt I was heading home anyway. I promised to spend the holidays with Mindy and that was the only thing in the world I wanted to do. I'd written her a song called, "Mindy, Will You Marry Me?" and I wanted to sing it to her at her sister's house on Christmas Eve in front of her family.

I missed her more than I had ever missed anything in my life and just wanted to be with her forever. I'd been working for sixteen to eighteen hours a day, every minute scheduled, and was just plain sacked out. When I got home from Pittsburgh on December 13, 1999, the same day I'd gotten there, I couldn't wait to see her. I'd been eating Parrillo Bars in the car the whole day though and my stomach was so cramped it hurt. I went around the corner of my house to urinate before going in so I wouldn't have to run immediately into the bathroom. I unzipped my pants, farted, and shit my pants. I dragged myself into the house, told her "honey, I'm sorry, I shit my pants, I'll be out in a little bit." I cleaned up, showered, and spent another fantastic; reunion styled evening with my girl.

The following morning I was due to go and pick up the two grand from Parrillo for the month of December. It was late, but I didn't care. I intended to use it for Christmas and to buy Mindy a ring. Hell, I'd spent well over two thousand dollars already getting Parrillo publicized and fully intended to spend more. My personal manager had already gotten his cut of it as I'd signed over the Vision Fit International check for four hundred over to him. I talked to Steve at Parrillos that day and he said he had bad news. I wasn't getting any money for the month because they simply didn't have it. They dropped several athletes due to unexpected expenses with the Y2K shit. I called and bitched at my personal manager who from that day has had no communication with me but to send all my promotional material back. Again, I was stupid to let someone communicate for me. I know I'm the best at it, and was simply being lazy not to be more up on it. The relationship did need to end, however, and I was now ready, as usual, to do what was necessary to ensure the development of another strategy to progress towards the goals I am determined to achieve.

Chapter 16
2000 The Master Plan

(Q)"Will the Naked Cowboy sing for just anybody?"

(A)"The Naked Cowboy doesn't see anybody as just anybody."

Christmas went fabulous. I gave Naked Cowboy boots, hats and other memorabilia to my loved ones as gifts. Symbols of the fact that my whole existence, and hard work, is primarily for them. I spent the holidays with Mindy as I promised her and wouldn't have had it any other way. I proposed to her and am committed to living the rest of my life with her as one team, working together to fulfill our missions. I've come to realize as a result of my loving her the way that I do, that she, in fact, strengthens me and makes me more formidable in fulfilling my destiny. Destiny is what she completes for me. I have been spending more and more time working at Fridays as a result of my massive efforts to get my financial house in tight order. I've come to realize, again, how important it is to be a worker and what a feeling of security it is to love work and know that loving it is paramount to a fruitful life. I fully intend to make hard work, at Fridays, a staple of my life because it gives me the ability to demonstrate a very serious work ethic for my closest peers and friends. I will be a millionaire by year's end and will have a limousine drive me to work where I will sweat balls to be the best singing, celebrity waiter on the planet who feels no need to live like a pampered movie star which I could easily emulate. I love my family dearly and my first work of order is to free my mother of debt, then my brother Kenny, then Andy, then humanity for the sake of them. I only want to give and to stand for giving. I hope that it is self evident that I want my girl, my love, my everything, Mindy, to have anything she wants and will seek to influence her in every way to want the same noble things that I have herein stated to want.

On Thursday, January 20, 2000, I went back to Hackettstown and this time stayed with my new friend Jim. He went with me into New York where, in three days, I managed to get airtime on Fox and Friends, the Today Show and Howard Stern. I sang and played for an hour in ten-degree weather with snow. Jim provided me with all accommodations and has professed to want to do such any time he can. In return, he has a most intriguing friend and fellow adventurer who daily designs the most extravagant life long adventure. Like everyone I've ever met who got to know me, he wants to be a part of my life. I've said it a thousand times to thousands of people, "if you can find a piece of the puzzle that you can do better than anyone else, the piece is yours to fill." I'm doing God's work and it's tough, loving, and accepting to all that seek to enlist. By God I will be "the most celebrated entertainer of all time." I will continue to give two hundred and ten percent because

I can. I am fiercely committed, fiercely determined. I will change myself countless times as I have done consistently over my life, and though I may not always seem to be sincere, I always am. You will see and know me as what I am, a bad ass, loving contributor who stands for determination!

Chapter 17
New York City Objective

"I am a slave to the impulse of communication that seeks to express itself through the written word."

Well I don't know how long it's been since I last declared where and what I was doing, but it couldn't have been too long cause my first journal entry since I put down this work was March 2, 2000. On this date I did a local radio interview on WAIF with Jimmy Miller, a friend who hosted it. I was there to talk about anything, a basic interview, and was gearing up for my next New York City trip for which I was to depart on March 7, 00. Getting kicked off of the major nighttime television talk shows had been a primary new agenda for me as no formal invitations to be on them had yet to come.

My friend Jim Richards in Hackettstown, taking on a greater and greater participatory role in my dream scape, had been working diligently through the internet to try and obtain tickets to be in the audience of any show he could find. The David Letterman Show, Conan O'Brian, Rosie O'Donnell, and several others were all likely targets. When I arrived in Hackettstown on March 7, 2000, I was nearly dead. I don't know if it was something I ate or just my usual exhaustion. I'd worked for roughly fifty hours a week on top of training like a madman in the gym each day and running at least once a day. I also did every local event that was hosted by a radio show in the city during the day. I left in my 84' Beamer in the early morning feeling great but was vomiting and dealing with diarrhea at every rest stop I could find from Cincinnati to New Jersey. When I arrived after thirteen hours of driving I crawled out of my car and Jim literally carried my weak, sickly two-hundred and twenty pound body up the steps of his apartment.

The following day was spent eating soup and recovering which consisted of super-sweaty sleeping under the sheets on his sofa-bed with serious cold chills. The next day we talked at length as to what was being done to obtain the nighttime show tickets and how long we might have to wait to get them. We did Fox and Friends as the Naked Cowboy and Times Square which got us on MTV.

On Friday, March 10, I sold Howard Stern fliers that Jim had made on his computer outside of Howard's studio on 57th street. I then went in and talked to K.C. Armstrong, the show's producer, about coming up with a song for Howard. We did Fox and Friends again and Times Square and got two separate news channels on the square which provided what I really wanted to feel; that the trip had really been worthwhile. Jim made awesome food and we shared as we always have, great food and conversation about how this whole Naked Cowboy thing was slowly, but surely, working out beautifully. We again confirmed that getting tickets to the nighttime talk shows was a great idea that would be pursued to completion.

I was home on March 11, 00 in Cincinnati but back on my way to Hackettstown again on March 20, 2000. I'd been working at Friday's only a week or so when Jim called to say he had a chance to get tickets to the David Letterman Show. We had to answer a question about the show in order to obtain the tickets. Neither Jim or I had really been TV watchers at all. In fact, at the time, neither of us even had one to watch. My good friend from Fridays, Drake the bartender, who incidentally knows everything, called the show and successfully answered the question that landed Jim and I in balcony seats at the Ed Sullivan Theater on March 22, 2000.

I had on home-made pants with Velcro lining and a loose shirt with boots on. My cowboy hat was in the bag Jim was carrying and no guitar would be needed for this 'brief' appearance. I was nervous only cause I didn't want to mess up what would surely be a one shot deal. Barbara Walters was Dave's guest and I thought about jumping up and interrupting but couldn't get my dad's words out of my mind. "It's as American as apple pie, you don't interrupt someone else while they're performing." I also remembered reading an article about David saying that he was extremely particular and that he spent several hours rehearsing every line and that he hated to mess up. With all this in mind I waited for the audience shot which consisted of a camera on a mechanical arm that scoped the entire crowd. When it did, I ripped off my clothes, walked down the aisle to the balcony rail, threw up my arms and waited til I was carted out by heavy security. I was talked to harshly and detained in the main lobby of the theater until CBS security decided what to do with me. They let me go hurling threats that I'd have "my ass sued off." I drove home from Hackettstown the next day worried that I'd really have legal trouble over this one and that I was going to have my plans hindered.

After fourteen hours of driving, I came home to Mindy at my apartment and I told her I was "going to be sued for millions of dollars." The phone then rang and it was Jim telling me that I was on the front page of CBS.com on the internet. It was a picture of me as the Naked Cowboy in the audience on the balcony of the Ed Sullivan Theatre with my arms up in the air with a hero's stance. The caption read, "thank Al Gore for his video editing machine. An impromptu performance at last night's show." I knew I was in the clear even though they had not aired it on the program. They couldn't possibly use me on their web site to their advantage and then sue me. All was well, and I again felt that I was on the greatest mission on the face of the earth.

On March 24, 2000 I was waiting tables again at Fridays and saving money for the next call from Jim to do whatever show he could get us tickets for. Mindy and I were having differences again which left my personal life empty but like every time before, I worked as hard as possible knowing in my heart that it would just be a matter of time before we were united again.

On Monday, April 3, 2000, I led the Red's Opening Day Parade in Cincinnati. I got news and radio coverage and was really treated quite nicely. When I got home from the parade I turned on the news and watched as they asked members of the crowd what they liked best about the parade. A little boy said "the cowboy," and a little girl said "guitar man." What did I tell you? I did several other events as well in Cincinnati. It was all just practice to me for my next trip to New York for which I left on April 10, 00. The itinerary consisted of The Howard Stern Show, The Rosie O'Donnell Show, which Jim had obtained tickets to over the internet, and Fox and Friends and the Today Show.

My arrival in Hackettstown on April 10, 00 was much better than the last one. I was tired as usual as I'd sought to make my time at home as productive and profitable as possible, but at least I went into Jim's apartment on my own two feet. I had had this great idea about a week prior- to go to The Howard Stern Show as the "Black Naked Cowboy." So I did just that. I painted my entire body black, put in a pair of buck teeth and went in claiming I was a "biness man, here to see Howard Stern." I also sang one of my hit songs, "Jerry Curl" for Robin, his African-American

104

co-host. I had to do one better than my last appearance which was the Naked Cowboy with the buck teeth acting just plain stupid and crazy. I also wanted to demonstrate a man so confident and accepting of the human condition that laughing at myself and others was not something I feared but enjoyed. My next appearance is going to be the Naked Cowgirl. People will call me a fag, a transvestite, whatever.

History and other bold men of today will see a man armed with courage destined to be the most amazing entertainer willing to belittle himself at all costs for his audience, the way the best entertainers do. I did Fox and Friends as the "Chocolate Naked Cowboy," a slight name change for a more conservative audience. I did the Today Show as my "Naked Cowboy Super-Hero." wearing red long-johns, top and bottom, underwear on top of them, and an American Flag for a cape. I was mentioned and aired without problems. Jim and I went to the Rosie O'Donnell show on day three of the trip. Instead of trying to jump out of the audience in my underwear like I did on Letterman, I decided to just get in line like everyone else as the "Naked Cowboy Super-Hero". All was going great. Everyone in line was excited and promising me victory. Next thing you know three guys in suits come up to me and say that my outfit is too flamboyant and that I have to go. This marked the end of the big-time talk show appearances for the time being as I began to wonder if it wasn't time to do another tour of the great USA.

That night Jim and I talked at length about the success
we did have and again of the coming victory that was
sure to be ours. Jim has taken to me and my dreams
like few have. Like a spiritual guide destined also to
play a major role in the rise of the Naked Cowboy.

I drove back to Cincinnati on March 14, 00 to an
empty apartment where I played guitar and sang to the
beautiful acoustics that rang free in the space between
fire-proof walls, the wood floors and the curtainless
bay windows. It was a quiet, empty place I could call
mine.

Chapter 18
Naked Cowboy Tour 2000

It was June, 5, 2000 when I got en route to cross the country again with a boat-load of Naked Cowboy underwear. I had rented a car for this trip and really don't know why it never occurred to me before to make arrangements to have reliable transportation to travel seven-thousand miles in twenty days. I'd called every radio show I'd been on and did an interview with all but one or two. I told them where and what I was doing again. Only two or three were on the route because I didn't really begin utilizing radio until my "Naked Cowboy East Coast Tour" which was of course a different route that traveled east. I did, however, e-mail radio shows in every city that I planned to go through and scheduled appearances in those that responded. I would simply show up at the radio stations' studios in cities that failed to jump at such a golden opportunity as to have such a star studded stud as myself at so cheap a rate- free. I did roughly thirty radio interviews prior to leaving Cincinnati and had eight scheduled before leaving on the fifth of June, which, in radio advertising dollars, considering the amount of time I had on air, nation-wide, would be worth millions to anyone with a product.

Just for the record, Parrillo Performance, whom I mentioned repeatedly in all my radio spots, gave me Parrillo Bars to eat and distribute for the entire trip.

The point of the trip was as it was on all previous trips, and in actuality, the reason I live, to get national news coverage. I would get on a radio morning show in each city I came to. I would find a way to get on the news in the afternoon, and if all went as had gone on all previous trips, I would get national news coverage by tour's end as a result of local clips being shown on the affiliates' national news outlets (Inside Edition, Access Hollywood, Entertainment Tonight, etc.).

I also had scheduled, prior to leaving, an appearance on "To Tell the Truth." -a new show, a recreation of an old show, that was being produced by NBC. It would be shot in Burbank, California, and I would be taken care of by the studio for my time in California. It was a "guaranteed" national appearance which would make the tour worthwhile if nothing else happened. Of course, you can't travel across the most amazing country in the world, singing and playing guitar in front of millions of un-suspecting people in the busiest cities after alerting their media without something happening. The person-to-person communication itself is legendary. The tour maps featuring the latest photo of the Naked Cowboy, well, let's just say that as I write this now, I know they're hanging in offices and homes in every corner of our nation. My diet was in proportion to my goals and outlook and that means it was strict. It had to fit into a financial budget, a mental box of lunacy, and be designed to make me ripped beyond belief. I'd gotten down to chicken breasts and fibrous veggies again, then switched to soy nuts. I'd only recently learned that soy nuts were in the world, and fell in love with them. I had every one in my personal sphere of influence eating them, and to eat them, with Parrillo Bars, exclusively, I could eat for two dollars a day plus water and coffee.

I got a tattoo of Jesus Christ on my left arm to add balance as I have had a tattoo of the devil on my right arm since the age of sixteen. To me, it was just a fresh paint job on the body of legend that would remain a mystery, like everything else in my life, for people to speculate about over the remainder of history. Mindy called and came over the day prior to me leaving and made my desire to take off, live in California or anywhere else along the way that invited sure stardom, seem frivolous. Instead I just wanted to get the hell home as quickly as possible to be with my one and only baby.

On June 5, 2000, I left Cincinnati from Mindy's new apartment in Glendale, Ohio and drove to Nashville. I left at two a.m. and arrived in Nashville around six a.m.. I went to the Opryland Hotel where I was to look for Bill Cody. He had a radio show. I did find him. I did get a two to three minute interview on air. Then I went to the city's interior where I waited outside of, and was ridiculed from inside of, "The Jerry House Foundation."-a local radio show. I was in no mood for dumb shit so I got in the car and drove to Birmingham, Alabama. I had only an e-mail confirmation from a guy who wasn't really in charge at the "Rick and Bubba Show" and so when I arrived at the Quality Inn that I have customarily stayed as a guest at when doing an appearance on their show, no reservation had been made. I was ready to go back to Cincinnati and scrap the whole damn thing but instead got into the Naked Cowboy gear and went to the studio knowing full well that they were off the air by now. When I went in, everyone- as usual -flipped out. Rick and Bubba and Speed Racer, the producer were all there and almost immediately with me. They had known nothing of Tour 2000 but were willing to have me for an interview the following day, book me a room at the Quality, and pretty much, just be cool as all hell to the Naked Cowboy.

I went to the Quality after that, called a few friends back home, and of course Mindy, then worked out like a titan in the hotel's work-out facility. I went to bed listening to some Earl Nightingale tapes and taking notes- actually on the whole series- which I would read over the following day as I drove to Baton Rouge. On June 6, 2000, I was on the Rick and Bubba Show. I was cool. They have a daily audience of over five million and are ever increasing in fame and popularity, which of course go hand in hand. They talked to me and made me part of the whole morning's program. I was taken around in the "Rick and Bubba Shuttle Bus" with Speed Racer to appear and be made a joke of at several Birmingham locations. I sang Rick and Bubba's breakfast order at a

Waffle House on air. I got to speak at length and make much better acquaintance with Speed Racer who is really a great guy with a great heart. He told me that radio was "the theatre of the mind." It was a perspective that would serve me in all my radio interviews hence forward.

It turns out that I was not in good standing with the Rick and Bubba Show and several of their audience members as a result of my last appearance with them at the "Rick and Bubba Fat Fest." It was there that I performed "Get Your Ass Kicked by a Man in His Underwear," a hit song by the Naked Cowboy, in front of five thousand plus Rick and Bubba Fans. They hadn't prepped me for the appearance, and I wasn't experienced enough to know how to read an audience of working-class Christian families. I apologized on air and certainly meant it. I'm so sincere at heart that I fail to realize at times that my simplicity and disregard for external appearances, sometimes comes across as shallow and callous. I remember Bubba saying, "we really didn't know what Cowboy would be singing, and when he was finished with his first number, we didn't know if we should pull him off or just let him continue the onslaught." That's funny now in retrospect, isn't it. I listen to a lot of radio, and Rick and Bubba really are, genuinely, funny. I finished and whole-heartedly thanked them for everything. I stopped in Historic Laurel, Mississippi, took off everything but my short shorts and shoes and jogged for forty minutes to build cardiovascular density and to get a tan. I passed out a few "Naked Cowboy Tour Maps" to a few stunned onlookers. Then drove to just outside of Baton Rouge where I worked out with the weights I'd brought with me in my rented room. Motel Six was my home for the night from which I made my calls before jogging and going to bed as usual. Soy nuts were eaten all day, with coffee, water and Parrillo Bars.

On June 7, 2000, I drove into Baton Rouge. This would be the first city on the tour with no scheduled radio morning show appearance. That simply meant that I'd have to make one up. I checked the Yellow Pages as I usually do, located the building with the most radio station addresses inside, listened to the call numbers on my radio to get the names of the d.j.'s, then went to the stations to see them. "Yeah, I'm here to see Bender and Maybe." "Wait here, I'll be right back, can I tell them who's here?" Yeah, I'm the Naked Cowboy." Two minutes later I'm in the building waiting to go on air.

In Baton Rouge I did three radio shows in the morning. I asked each of them what was the biggest thing going on in the town. The best that I could come up with was a legislative hearing at the capitol building. It was the last day for the legislature to come up with a fiscal debt solution that pertained, I believe, to the salaries of a whole lot of police officers and other city administrators. I went to the capitol building, and went inside where hundreds of suit-and-tie people were gathered. News crews were setting up inside a room that was blocked off and where I would not be able to enter and there was a team out front on the steps leading to the entrance. I went into the bathroom, got into Naked Cowboy attire and came out of the bathroom, through the halls of the capitol building singing, "I'm the Naked Cowboy coming to a town near you!" Of course everyone was dumbfounded and wondering what the hell I was doing there. I went through the crowd, made my way out the front door and down the front steps in front of the cameras. I was grabbed by police and led to my car. I then left Baton Rouge and headed for Houston. I ran in the sun just outside of Houston, worked out with my weights, and made phone calls and ate more damn soy nuts.

On June 8, 2000, I was in Houston, cussing up a storm, unable to get reliable directions to the radio station. I guess traveling the country would be easier with a map. I did finally find it. I remember the D.J. Larry Moon, saying that "I'm sorry, I'm having trouble getting you on, our program generally doesn't allow for anyone who is not on the cover of People Magazine." I told him to tell the program director that I was working on it. Like every other radio show I've done, do, and will do, they loved me and said that the segment was fabulous and very funny. They said that I could come back at any time and I said they could count on it. They used a webcam like most of them do, especially with me ,and they took promotional pictures with me, at every radio show in the place, to show everyone-" hey look, the Naked Cowboy was in our studio." I then circulated all over Houston looking for a place to play to get the news. I was getting a little discouraged cause the city all of the sudden seemed larger than I remembered it and I just didn't want to call the news and hear them say they weren't interested. I couldn't find anyone who knew of anything that was going on either. I went into the Houston Chronicle where Rad Sallee did an article on me on my first tour. He was not available and told the secretary in the front lobby that he'd try to get a reporter on it if I'd disclose the location where I'd be performing. The next time that reporter saw me would have been on the news, on both of Houston's main channels-being arrested for performing in front of the Criminal Justice building. I'd seen the news truck out front and knew that the police would see my performance as a bit of an unnecessary tease. County property is usually more restricted than city. I was seen in handcuffs being led away by two officers towards the jail as I chanted, "I'm being arrested for playing guitar in my underwear." I also said, "hi mom!" At the holding tank I made good friends with the arresting officers as they told me of all the places they had seen me on TV including their local news on previous trips. They, and their superiors, came to really like me and got the man who was going to sign the statement of complaint against me to decide differently. It was a long process however, and I spent close to three hours handcuffed to a church pew in the holding facility as hoards of officers came by the window to see me.

At least two dozen opened the door to make small talk to the officers doing my paper work. When the man in charge of everything came to say that we're letting you out knowing" you won't come back on county property." I was led out by a team of officers, again before news cameras. They were waiting outside to get an interview and got one at the trunk of my car as I held up Parrillo Bars saying, "eat like the Naked Cowboy, be built like the Naked Cowboy."

How cool is that? The news was waiting for me to be released to get an interview. Must have been a terribly slow news day. I drove to the Scottsman Hotel just outside of San Antonio. It was a long ride and I was tired as all hell, so I did what I always do. I ran, worked out, read serious loads of self-help material ("Unlimited Power," my "Ideal Day," and my "personal beliefs and value hierarchy), before making calls, and eating more damn soy nuts. Oh, and hell, yes all these freakin' nuts were doing a number on my stomach as I was by now able to make musical numbers with my rear end.

Journal Entry 6//8/00

I feel fame coming over me! Everywhere that I go I am the awesome center of attention! I'm persistent like Emerson's "Hero" and so I am becoming a recognizable hero! The ripple I began in the ocean of humanity is rapidly approaching the shoreline! I am a tidal wave of unprecedented service and greatwill! Thank-you God for the privilege to do your work.

On June 9, 2000, I was on the "Drex and Roberta Show" in San Antonio, Texas. This was the most liberal show I'd heard so far as they cussed and talked about anal sex and all kinds of alternative crazy stuff that I'd really not heard ever on radio outside of the "Howard Stern Show." They had transvestites and gay men and one straight woman named Roberta. I was driven around town by Roberta. She took me to a busy intersection where I sang and played guitar amidst a great deal of traffic. It was drizzling and so I looked about as ridiculous as all hell. People honked and shook their heads as people took pictures. I got two newspapers and two other radio stations brought their trucks up to interview me on air. It was no big deal to me to be playing guitar in my underwear in the rain on the median of a busy intersection. I was just getting in my days practice at being the "most celebrated entertainer of all time" with a good deal of advertising at the same time. The news crew didn't get to me until I'd gotten back to the radio station. They shot me playing in the studio and interviewed me at length in the hall of the radio station. I was assigned a reporter that came to the San Antonio "Riverwalk" to follow me through what we felt would be loads of people. However, it was raining. The cameraman, Jimmy, and I, sought desperately to find a location where anyone was present. No people means no reaction and really, no big deal.

We ended up at the world famous Alamo where hundreds of little kids and tourists were running wild. He waited on one side of the street while I went across the street into a restaurant to change into persona. I put on the portable microphone he gave me, busted out singing and just plain tore the place up. People screamed and chanted Naked Cowboy as the cameras flashed like mad. The hoards of little kids laughed so loud you couldn't hear anything but their laughter. We got great footage, and did the high five accordingly. He took me back to the parking lot where my car was and I ran in pouring rain to my car while a couple of teenagers who I nearly stomped as I ran by called me a faggot. I was so glad to have made the cut with the news and gotten what I know would be great coverage.

I drove for a hell of a long time to El Paso and did another radio interview on the way as I was paged by the same station that had me on in the morning. As I drove I had passing notions of skipping El Paso and Phoenix and anything else between where I was and California. I wanted to save any money I could and felt that only one clip would make it national anyhow. I felt after the whole week of coverage, at least one would do it. I didn't want to spend two days doing nothing in El Paso waiting for Monday either, which is when my next scheduled appearance would be.

El Paso was a long drive in itself though, and when I did finally get there, I did just want to crash and burn for a while. I stayed at the Americana Inn Friday night, Saturday and Sunday. I laid out at the pool each day, worked out with my weights, read a lot, called everyone and sent postcards to my friends all over the world, and made arrangements with Mindy for her to fly out to California to make the trip back to Cincinnati with me.

I'd spoken to Colby from "To Tell the Truth," as they were keeping a careful eye on me to make sure I was still progressively making way to their studios in Burbank. I kept them informed and updated and they all shared my excitement as I was kicking some serious media ass. I do have to admit though, that no matter what success I'd seemed to have in the mornings and throughout the day, I felt like a loser who had nothing going for him by nightfall. I guess it's like a drug for me to be in the center of attention. When people are interviewing you and you know you're being heard, potentially worldwide, and then you go from that to being by yourself in a car in the middle of the desert, thousands of miles from anyone you really know... it's a serious range of emotional

119

extremes. It is for me at least, as I love without reservation the one, and hate the other.

On Monday, June 12, 2000, I drove into old familiar El Paso. It seemed very "hometown" to me. Maybe it's because I had been there two or three times already, and because while waiting out the weekend at the Americana Inn, I went in for a little dry run to see where things were. Either way, it seemed familiar to me. I went straight to the studio of Mike McKay at Cat Country 94.7 and was immediately put on air. He and his co-host were extremely cool and willing to help me get the media. I was taken to the news room itself, Channel 4, and did a piece outside the afternoon show with Mike. I was also taken to a busy intersection where a news camera tried to keep up with me as I walked in between high speed traffic singing. It was my most dangerous appearance to date, but with cameras watching my every move, I knew the worse I got, the further the news would travel. I did an interview on air and then drove all the way to Phoenix. Thank God before I left I was able to find a natural health store where I got four pounds of soy nuts. I had just ran out and was getting nervous as they were the foundation upon which my current life's objective were based. The drive seemed extremely long as did the hour long run in the desert and even my time out to read and tan. I did the mantra over and over in my mind as I drove, "capacity is a state of mind."

On Tuesday morning, I got up just outside of Phoenix in a hotel room to seedy to carry a sign out front and drank a "Ripped Fuel." It's a sports drink with Ephedrine in it. I hadn't had one in so long that it worked like it never has before. Got my heart racing so fast I skipped Phoenix and drove all the way to California. All I did all day was drive. Literally from sun up to sun down. I called my friend Ken Beck in Hollywood and asked if he would leave the door open. I got there at approximately two a.m. and crawled into bed as he was not there. I was so tired I could have slept on a bed of nails.

Goal Setting Exercises 6/12/00
(Written while driving across New Mexico)

I want to be the indisputably best built, most beautiful man in history. I want every last person on this planet to be able to recognize me instantly. I want to be honored consistently as a hero of determination, commitment and honor. I want to be world renowned for my unquestioned level of love and service to humanity. I want to develop my mind so that I am truly and consistently at peace with myself and all of humanity and all creatures. I want my voice and words to be as recognizable and loved as my image, message, and reputation. I want to be a celebrated communicator of success, achievement and love beyond reproach. I want my photo, and images, and life story to be one to emulate for all time. I want the ability to say what is right in all situations and to get results from kings and pawns. I want talent and opportunity equal to my drive and persistence. I want perfection to be conditioned and automatic. I want these glorious things to be concentrated in me so powerfully that they radiate from me in every instant of my life. I want them to radiate outward from me and to effect humanity and all of nature. I want this powerful aura to attract the world to me so that I can praise and thank all and everything as it comes into my presence. I want all of these circumstances I have herein stated to begin or continue to manifest themselves in my life now! I want to and will attract as I project. The evidence will be massive continued success in unequaled snowballing publicity and talk about me, my goals, my objectives, my story, and mostly my actions. Sponsors, book deals, record deals, endorsements, financial abundance unparalleled in the annals of history, mass hysteria at my appearance, devotion by all loved ones and friends and acquaintances and onlookers. All is and has been occurring and now with my continued focus and persistent actions, the rush will captivate the world.

On 6/13/00 I awoke in one of my future worldwide hideaways, Hollywood, California. It was already late morning and so morning shows were out and I really just wanted a day to relax. I was exhausted as soon I got out of bed. The sun was shining and so I went out on the patio with a cup of soy nuts and basked in the sun for over an hour. I read "Unlimited Power," and with that was ready to go like never before.

I went down to Hollywood Boulevard and played guitar singing as the Naked Cowboy through crowds of tourists. I got on camera and was aired the same night on the local news. I worked out, swam and ran and did a host of mental exercises on paper to sharpen my focus. When Ken got home we had a few drinks, watched movies and talked about anything and everything.

On 6/14/00 I was hungry as all hell for something of California's enormous broadcast area. I went first to KZLA which is California's number one country station. I jumped their security fence and was declined initially but then chased down to return after that. I received incredible coverage as they let their listening audience decide if I could come on. They talked of people who were famous just for being famous and that they felt it was a good thing. Just to clarify, I'm not just going to be famous, regardless of why I am, I'm going to be the most famous. I drove all around Southern California looking for media of any kind finally returning to Hollywood Boulevard again to entertain tourists. I spent the evening again with Ken and one of his, and now my, good friends, Brandon. We had drinks and watched the movie, "South Park" and I can't believe that movie is legal.

On 6/15/00 I was turned down by KLOS, the "Mark and Brian Show." It was no big deal but I have nothing else to say about the day.

On 6/16/00 I went on a radio rampage. I got on 98 Rock (via phone) in Maryland, I did the "Jamie and Danny Show" in Burbank, I did the "Rick Dee's Show" in Burbank too. I got what I wanted from all of these shows just by showing up and refusing any outcome other than to be aired. I then went to NBC Studios to pick up my hotel room keys and to speak with Colby, one of the show's producers who'd been keeping tabs on me as I crossed the country. I did this as the Naked Cowboy and got purposely" lost" on the studio grounds to make certain the entire place was talking about me. I checked into the Burbank Hilton and hit the Jacuzzi before working out, tanning, and taking a long nap which ended up being a long night's sleep.

Saturday, 6/17/00 would be another history making day for the Naked Cowboy. After some forty days and forty nights of nearly nothing but soy nuts, I taped "To Tell the Truth" as the Naked Cowboy. It was done a day early as we were asked to come in and be on stand-by for an extra hundred dollars. It was me and two other guys also claiming to be the Naked Cowboy. I was very, very, very ripped and as awesome as a Naked Cowboy should be. Some of my finest work. The publicity was truly encouraging and fantastic as millions of people worldwide will see in mid September of 2000. It was the biggest reason for the tour, and a defining moment in the country wide stretch. I prepared, I'd done just under two years of work to make it happen, and it was done and a stellar job to say the least. It's never been done and that is why the focus of the coverage was, "this man is famous for singing in his skivvies." I'd given the extra room key to the hotel clerk to give to Mindy when she arrived at the hotel and she was waiting in my room when I got there after the show taped. Another cosmic match made in history was under way and time was not even a consideration. We went out to eat and sat in our hot tub with "Sour Apple Schnapps" at night's end.

On 6/18/00, Mindy and I did the Boardwalk. We started at the Santa Monica Pier eating at "Cocina Mexican Marisol" and then walked all the way down to Venice along the Boardwalk. It was probably a four to five mile walk. We took in the sites as we had done on previous trips. We got lots of sun and had a great time. We spent the afternoon again in the hot tub drinking, this time, "Captain Morgans" and coke and retired early.

When Monday rolled around, the tour was really over for me. I scheduled radio shows on the way back across the country, but two out of three called to cancel, one for the "Dixie Chicks," and another for "programming complications." I'd said to myself several times prior, "just get to California, do the show, get anything possible along the way, and only those appearances that were scheduled, along the way back." It was in my plans to make a sort of "makeshift honeymoon type" arrangement with Mindy on the way back. I'd worked hard as dog shit on the way out and knew that I had done what was necessary to send a vibe across humanity. I knew we'd have a bearable time, driving another three to four thousand miles in five days, if I took the pressure off, and we did. In fact, we had some awesome times. We spent two hours, on three days, scaling mountainous terrain, flat-land desert, and a mixture of both. We made love in the great outdoors and while driving eighty on open highway. We saw America together again and bonded like two only can when at arm's length through difficulty. Not difficulty in a bad sense, but the kind of difficulty that builds character and strength. We had our rendezvous with nature and with each other. It was another intense period in our lives that would serve to strengthen our knots of togetherness for a lifetime. We did stop however, in Salt Lake City for Naked Cowboy business, where together we got three news channels, and one newspaper. We arrived home on 6/23/00 after a morning radio interview on the "Randy Miller Morning Show" in Kansas City. I had driven a total of six-thousand miles in eighteen days!

Chapter 19
ABC News Break

I was only home a week and a day, worked my ass off nonstop at Fridays and then left again for Hackettstown on 7/2/00. I had this idea to be on the Howard Stern Show again, this time as the Naked Cowgirl. I would wear Mindy's pink bikini, and make-up, and go in singing.

Well, it was July 4th weekend and the whole radio show was on vacation. I decided to do the crapshoot on Times Square-to play as the Naked Cowboy and see who pays a damn bit of attention. I got on MTV's "Total Request Live," and then got an interview with

Lara Spenser of ABC News. That clip was aired on television stations from one end of the country to the other. I got calls from California and New York, and friends in my hometown of Cincinnati, Ohio saw it at four A.M., on world news. I also received a call from a radio show I'd been on in Meridian, Mississippi who saw the clip on CNNSI, another national venue. It was awesome coverage.

I returned to Cincinnati where I worked eighteen out of twenty days in a row, at approximately ten hours a night. I made money and prepared for whatever my internal urges told me to do next. It again said Howard Stern. On Wednesday, July 26 2000, I successfully got rejected by the "Howard Stern Show" as the Naked Cowgirl. I will be aired, I'm very confident as the Naked Cowgirl, on E! as a result of the visit. Tomorrow will be Thursday, and I will make yet another appearance as a Gorilla, in underwear, boots, hat and guitar. "Damn, this guy will stop at nothing," On July 27, 00 I went and got successfully rejected by the "Howard Stern Show" again, this time as the Naked Gorilla."

Unlike every other time I've been rejected however, this time I got a return date to appear on the "Howard Stern Show" as the Naked Cowboy for an interview. The date was set or September 6, 2000, which will give me the opportunity to promote my NBC appearance on "To Tell the Truth," which will also air the same month. These two performances, coupled with what has already been done and mentioned above, should provide a hefty spark in making the "Naked Cowboy" a household name by year's end.

Chapter 20
National Nobody Turns International Nobody!!!

The year two thousand came and went and I tried desperately as you have read to become a house hold name by 2000's end. What does that mean to me? Well I guess it would mean that everyone in the human race would have a "reasonable" chance of hearing about a very determined man in America who runs around the country to fulfill his dreams in his underwear. A tale, no pun intended, of a spiritual presence seeking to harness its human experience to serve as a metaphor for the unlimited possibilities each one of its equally loved and admired spirits possesses.

Although I haven't written anything that I felt was worth reading since September, 1999, some five months ago, I can assure you the intensity of my actions and focus only progressed and my desire doubled. The events that I made happen over this time period can be observed at the Trail Of Events link at nakedcowboy.com.

Something rather extraordinary did occur in my life though, I must admit, on January 22, 2001. CNN, out of New York City, aired an interview I taped with them on January 3, 2001. That news piece, which lasted two minutes and twenty nine seconds, was featured on their program across the entire world!!! It was then dished out to over four hundred new networks, affiliates, college channels, local channels across the human race!!! To be fair to me and my efforts, after observing my e-mails that now come from nearly every country I can name in Europe, Canada, Asia, South America, Africa, and again, the great USA (the one country where just such dreams are made), I think it is "reasonable" to predict that by February's end (2001), every person in the human race could have at least heard of the Naked Cowboy.

So what now is the mission of the Naked Cowboy? Well let me just say that fulfilling my goal, almost, I did miss the mark by a couple of months, was secondary to what I have learned throughout my journey thus far. What I have learned is just exactly what I knew when I began. I learned it again, and again, and again. I will never be the "most celebrated entertainer of all time" until I can learn to value most, the things that are most valuable: Friendship, sincerity, family, honesty, compassion, humility, respect, and most of all love. All of the tools with which I have sought passionately to command. I can tell you from the bottom of my heart that I believe I have failed miserably in several of these areas several times and yet just by concentrating on improving in each area consistently, I've come to where I am now still! I will live to be the "most celebrated entertainer of all time" and I will promise you now that my level of determination will make what I have already done seem insignificant. I have been humbled what seems like an infinite number of times by the generosity of those who have allowed me to move forward with their blessings and now that I am in demand, I will humble myself infinitely to move ever so persistently forward for them. If, however, I have to designate one reason why I have been so willing and able to succeed and grow in this here depicted journey, it is because I believe in myself.

Destination Super-Stardom

When I was roughly seventeen years old, only days after stepping foot into Gold's Gym and working out for the first time, I came across a book called "Unlimited Power," by Anthony Robbins. It has been my definitive bible ever since. Within that book lies all of the secrets to unlocking the human potential and making men out of children. I could speak volumes as to what this book has done for me in my own spiritual mission in this world, but will leave it to you to take me at my word when I say it is pure magic and indispensable for one's personal growth and development.

One of the crucial things it has done for me:

I'm reading it now for the eighteenth time- was to steer me in the direction of my destiny. My inborn birthright, my inherent destiny as the "most celebrated entertainer of all time" was awaiting since birth to be released into the world. My inexhaustible capacity, stamina and obsessions were lying dormant and ready when this Anthony Robbins gave me the road map to channel it to super-stardom. It has several exercises that have served to continually push me further and further along my path of unquestionable action. The most important of which is called the "Ideal Day." This is the exercise where you write out everything you want, deserve, and will take no less than. It's where you create your most sought after outcome imaginable. You create a target that is fit for the divinity that you, in fact, are. Once you create your target, and write it out, and internalize it, you read it every day. You rehearse it over and over again and move yourself daily towards the realization of it. You make it your supreme life's endeavor to live it. I read mine every day and will live it as sure as you will live yours.

Ideal Day

I will awake totally refreshed and vibrant after a long night's rest. The oceans, the mountains, the forests and the deserts will be near my door. I will be in a king-sized bed or larger in the company of my beloved, living in one of my castles overlooking one of the world's most beautiful landscapes. The sun will be shining through my large bay windows, and cool ocean breezes will shake the curtains before drifting past my world-renowned, beautiful body. I will awake my loving companion with kisses and compliments in mutual love and harmony before setting onward into another day of bliss and reward. I will exit my beautifully furnished living quarters each morning after a glass or two of mountain spring water to exercise and stretch my beautifully shaped muscles. Nature will abound and abide to my deepest, truest aspirations and temperament. I will return to my castle to enjoy my loving companions company over a well-prepared, delicious breakfast. All of the world's delicacies will pass over my breakfast table. Each day's itinerary will be designed by me. My activities will have to be chosen amongst my own personal list of the "best of the best." My exciting work for each day will be paid with incredible funds and miraculous enjoyment. The amount of work that I do will be of my choosing and I will have the utmost earned respect of all those working with me. My work will create and provide astounding benefits and happy reward to everyone who witnesses it and everyone will witness it. Everywhere that I go I will be instantly recognized and respected. I will be known by all to be the most famous, wealthiest, loving man alive. People will request to have my autograph and photos taken with me everywhere. They will be inspired by my sensuality, charm, faith, confidence, determination, dedication, perseverance, courage, expectation, immeasurable good-looks, kindness, honesty, love and sincerity. My family members will be in frequent contact to wish each other well and to say hello. My family members will know unlimited wealth and expectation. I will eat in the very finest restaurants, hotels, lounges, casinos and other establishments of my choosing with my family members, friends, and companion for each meal as I choose. Reservations will always be made in advance or accepted with great pride and respect upon entering. I will stroll the beaches of the world: rest in its lagoons. I will lie under the world's most remarkable waterfalls and will bask regularly in the warm sun on every continent. Any amount of money that I spend on any given day will be o.k. I will never need to feel, in any way, financially restricted. I will know that on any given day, my wonderful family, friends, and supporters will have all that they want as a result of our association. I will give, give, give, and give again. I will share, care and love with all my might. I will travel to any part of the world that I wish at any given time with an unlimited number of excellent options to go, expenses paid, by loving people requesting my presence for work, friendship, meals, honoring, etc…. This beautiful world will truly be my rewarding playground. My gorgeous, loving family, friends, companion and supporters will be able to see this beautiful world as a result of their association with me. They will know no boundaries. I will work out in health clubs, the very finest of facilities, and will be immediately recognized and respected for having the finest, most refined body on the planet. My image will be one of complete happiness, love and success. I will be known by all to be serious and intense in the gym as well as curious and helpful. I will relax frequently in saunas and whirlpools, Jacuzzi, etc… Tranquil relaxation will always be in me. My great wealth will afford me the unique opportunity to be extremely well versed in all aspects of the theatre, opera, geography, business, music, arts, sciences, politics, culture, health, society and people. I will see all and do all as I choose, always being able to relax and enjoy what my tremendous accomplishments have returned to me. All sports and recreational activities will be open to me. I will scuba dive the depths of the oceans and jet ski their surfaces. I will free-fall from the highest altitudes and scale the highest mountains, all with my friends and family. All luxuries, whether sports car, sail boat, jet ski, yacht, airplane, helicopter or other assets, will be easily within my grasp.

At night I will be in the loving company of anyone I wish to enjoy the most exquisite locations and scenes the world has to offer, as will all those who are in close association with me. I will always return to one of my comfortable beds, refreshed and secure with my loving companion's heart in unity with mine. We will share an enduring love that will never lack trust, faith, honesty, sincerity and fidelity. Our respect for each other will be unselfish and unvarnished and we'll always be forgiving toward each other. I will both awake and go to sleep feeling energetic, wealthy, healthy, secure and excited about the day. I will never let adversity hold me back, but will maintain a sharp and clear, level head and take positive actions. I will always accentuate the positive and eliminate the negatives. I will read and relax whenever I choose and will see editorial photos, prints, commercials, movies, internet advertising, magazine covers, billboards and every other medium of advertisement and communication bearing my image whenever I look for them. I will be able, on any given day, to frequent my accounts, and properties and find that they only grow larger no matter how much my family my companion or I spend. The spirit of giving will run free in me and all that I touch. My life will emanate complete love and unimaginable happiness from every direction. I will be massaged by a masseuse upon my request as often as I want and will be able to shower, swim or just lay back alone whenever I want. The world's most fabulous resorts will be my weekly hideaways. The excitement of the world's largest airports will be included in my weekly itinerary. "Lifestyles of the Rich and Famous" will seek constantly to report my daily adventures. Peace and tranquility will be mine for eternity. All who know me will be lavished with astounding friendship, concern, assets, love and guidance if they believe I can give it to them, and happiness to know they have a true friend in me. Anyone and everyone who has ever so much as wanted to be of help or assistance to me shall be rewarded a thousand times over if they wish to be assertive enough to pursue it. I will be extremely charitable to all and willing to lend an abundance of time, money and effort to all causes or missions that are worthy and deserving. I will own anything I want but will never squander it for selfish interests. I will harness an attitude of simplistic elegance and enduring love, passion and contribution. I will know on any given day that I have the proudest friends, family and companion in the world. My loving co-workers, employees and associates in every major business will respect my ambition, drive and willingness to accept being the best. I will strive for all the entire world has to offer and get it. I will never fail to find happiness in my journey to and my arrival at the top!

I will know and feel completely confident on any given day that I am the most recognized and loved talent in the world, but will always be humble and never pompous or arrogant or demeaning to other aspirants. I will encourage all to shoot for the stars. My determined and unquestioned belief in the pursuit of my dream will spark millions to do likewise. The domino effect of my courage, desire, and ultimate actions and accomplishments will change the very character of the world. My loving managers, agents, photographers, planners, press agents, etc. will be fabulously wealthy, recognized throughout the world and respected for having zealously represented me. Their beautiful names will turn to gold. I will receive every honor known to man and I will deserve it. Love will radiate from my being for eternity. My love for life, my dedication and hard work for excellence, my compassion and open-mindedness will be world-renowned, recognized and sought after, if not emulated by all. Where I am the paparazzi will flock! I will be a damn good person to everybody, in spite of race, creed, religion, sex, sexuality, etc…. I will love, love, love, love, and love! I will be miraculously tolerant and accepting toward everyone. I will never forget that "to know all is to forgive all." I will never be purposely judgmental, but will accept everyone as part of my loving family. My perfected life story will be accepted, respected, revered and never challenged or second-guessed by anyone. People worldwide will admire the skill, intelligence and freedom that my goals have delivered to me. They will know only of the open-mindedness, the challenges met, battles won, hearts won, attitudes changed, message of love, desire for acceptance and obsessive dedication delivered; the self-sacrifice of all one has, had or would have for the purpose of achieving one's goals, desires, mission and destiny. My life story will be among the world's all-time best sellers of motivational and self-help books. They will start landslides of effort among all that read them and live their principles. They'll know and recognize the unselfish and determined effort to be a communicator or success and accomplishment to humanity. They'll recognize sacrifice for gain, great sadness and deprivation for gain, freedom in thought and acceptance of the true meaning of purpose despite hardship. In essence, a destined communicator of will and its ability to overcome any and all, bit by bit, with the entirety in mind, body and spirit. A loving message communicated worldwide by one determined man in the human condition with the truly exciting realization that this fortunate condition is determinable only by oneself and his desire to do so. They'll find this loving message: that no limit can stand in one's way unless allowed; that all inhibitions and limits are self-imposed; and that we all live in an undaunted realm of unlimited possibility.

My ideal day will be engrossed with exciting bright colors and sounds and feeling of exhilaration. These will all be complimented with soft, delicate, peaceful and serene sounds, sights of elegance and calmness and feelings of passion and tingling. Every fiber of my senses will be refreshed, sight, sound, taste and feeling. My mind, body and spirit shall remain in complete unity with all else for eternity. On my ideal day I will not forget to thank God, my loving creator, who has truly blessed me, for the courage, the discipline, the dedication, the drive, the ambition, the stamina, the might, the character, the personality, the audacity, the imagination, the values, the conditioning, the environment, the genetics, the freedom, the liberty, the riches, the right, the resources, the purpose, the spontaneity, the vision, the obedience, the ingenuity, the charisma, the belief systems, the technology, the family, the desire, the talent, the flexibility, the strength, the balance, the congruence, the assistance, the wisdom, the power, the attitude, the love, the grace, the kindness, the generosity, the sincerity, the friendships, the guidance, the help, the opulence, the serenity, the intelligence, the wit, the simplicity, the experience, the principles, the endurance the latitude, the faith, the complexity, the integrity, the beauty, the elegance, the manners, the states, the syntax, the metaprograms, the communication, the character traits, the commitment, the understanding, the empathy, the paradigms, the leadership, the magic, the fuel, the action habit, the rapport, the anchors, the charm, and the happiness with which I have created this life of my dreams. All praise and honor to our wonderful, loving God who nurtures our deepest, truest intentions.

"Gotta Do Whatcha Gotta Do!!!"

The End

Conclusion

To provide a general idea of how one man's determination can bring itself to fruition, a complete list of every day of Naked Cowboy's life can be found on his website under the title "Trail Of Events". This day by day account is updated monthly and is accurate back to 1997:

nakedcowboy.com/trailofevents.html

On December 10, 2008 Burck was officially registered as a marriage officiant by the City of New York after becoming an Ordained Minister.

As the popularity of Naked Cowboy grew, Burck began to make appearances on television, in music videos, and on other popular media. He auditioned for *American Idol* during its first season, but was not advanced to the next round. He also tried out for *Australian Idol* and *Star Search*, but with the same results. In 2000, he was on the short-lived show *Moral Court*, where conservative talk show host Larry Elder ruled that, in his opinion, Burck's Naked Cowboy persona was not immoral and not a danger to public safety. Burck replied, "Actually, I think I am an inspiration to public safety." On January 24, 2009, Burck also appeared on the *Tubridy Tonight* show on Ireland's RTÉ television network, performing his theme song "I'm The Naked Cowboy" accompanied by the Camembert Quartet. There have been discussions of possible television show concepts with several production houses, including Eric Bischoff of Bischoff Hervey Entertainment. There currently is a *Naked Cowboy Reality* series that can be found on YouTube produced by Ron Israel.

Here are Burck's Celebrity Credentials from IMDB:

Survive This (2005) .... The Naked Cowboy

Der Schein trügt (2009) .... Himself

Black Mold Exposure (2009) .... Himself

"The Apprentice" .... Himself (2 episodes, 2004-2009)
... aka "Celebrity Apprentice" - USA
... aka "The Apprentice 2" - USA
... aka "The Apprentice Los Angeles" - USA
... aka "The Celebrity Apprentice" - USA
- Episode #8.1 (2009) TV episode .... Himself
- Ethics Shmethics (2004) TV episode (uncredited) .... Himself

"Xposé" .... Himself (1 episode, 2009)
- Episode #3.93 (2009) TV episode (as Robert Burck) .... Himself

"Le grand journal de Canal+" .... Himself
- Episode dated 4 November 2008 (2008) TV episode .... Himself

The Genius of Charles Darwin (2008) (TV) .... Himself

"Law & Order: Criminal Intent" .... Himself
... aka "Law & Order: CI" - USA
- Vanishing Act (2008) TV episode .... Himself

Science of Horror (2008) .... Himself

"Today" .... Himself (1 episode, 2008)
... aka "NBC News Today" - USA (promotional title)
... aka "The Today Show" - USA (alternative title)
- Episode dated 25 June 2008 (2008) TV episode .... Himself

Meet Dave (2008) .... Himself

"Cristina's Court" .... Himself (1 episode, 2008)
- Episode dated 2 January 2008 (2008) TV episode .... Himself

"Big Time" .... Himself (1 episode, 2004)
... aka "Steve Harvey's Big Time" - USA
... aka "Steve Harvey's Big Time Challenge" - USA
- Episode #2.4 (2004) TV episode .... Himself

New York Minute (2004/I) (uncredited) .... Himself

Creature Feature: 50 Years of the Gill-Man (2004) (V) .... Himself

"Lonely Planet" .... Himself (1 episode, 2003)
... aka "Globe Trekker" - USA
- New York 2 (2003) TV episode (as John Robert Burck) .... Himself

"Troma's Edge TV" (2000) TV series .... Himself (unknown episodes, 2001)

American Icon (2001) (as John Robert Burck) .... The Naked Cowboy

Mulva: Zombie Ass Kicker! (2001) (V) .... Himself

"Howard Stern" .... Himself (3 episodes, 1999-2000)
- Episode dated 3 October 2000 (2000) TV episode .... Himself
- Episode dated 7 February 2000 (2000) TV episode .... Himself
- Episode dated 16 November 1999 (1999) TV episode .... Himself

"The Howard Stern Radio Show" .... Himself (3 episodes, 1999-2000)
- Episode dated 20 May 2000 (2000) TV episode .... Himself
- Episode dated 15 January 2000 (2000) TV episode .... Himself

- Episode dated 13 November 1999 (1999) TV episode .... Himself

Burck has also been featured in numerous corporate advertising campaigns. In 2006 he was part of USA Network's "Characters Welcome" campaign, and he also appeared in a Chevrolet commercial that aired during Super Bowl XLI, as well as a Guinness advertisement that aired only in the United Kingdom and Ireland, a Pepsi commercial with Beyoncé directed by Spike Lee and several TV commercials for MTV and VH-1.

Burck currently has 10 active corporate endorsement/licensing deals with:

* **ConstantLink.com**

* **The Times Square Vistor's Center**
* **Blue Island Shellfish Farms (Naked Cowboy Oysters)**
* **Anthony Ruiz Photography**
* **Kaufman Furs**
* **Vodafone**
* **Joseph Abboud**
* **Tour Supply**
* **Parillo Performance**
* **Hudson Hair**

Burck has also made appearances in several music videos, including Cake's "Short Skirt/Long Jacket" and Nickelback's "Rockstar". In 2007, Burck released two albums of his own, signing two independent record deals. One with 4Sight Music Productions recording the pop-rock album "Year of the Cowboy" produced by Lee Evans and Gaetano Lattanzi at

JAMBOX Recording Studios in New York City and the second with TMR Records recording the country music album "What The Naked Cowboy Wants To Hear" which I produced for my label at my studio, TMR Productions, The Funhouse and The Tracking Room recording studios in Nashville, TN. We just finished producing his second album for TMR Records called "X-Rated Country" which officially released on December 7th, 2010.

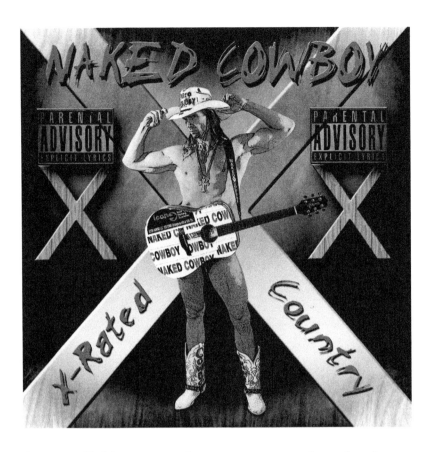

CDs available at xratedcountry.com or download at your favorite digital distributive retail outlet.

Naked Cowboy has had increasing significant success as a world known media icon representing New York City and Times Square with Network Premiers, News Stories, Radio Interviews, Press Releases, Political Events, Live Shows, TV Shows, Music Videos, "Grate Performances" for the Times Square Alliance in conjunction with Event Networks and merchandising sales at the Times Square Visitor's Center, Major Motion Pictures, TV Commercials, etc., etc.

Naked Cowboy has been declared by the New York State tourism department as "more recognizable than The Statue of Liberty", he's been named "The Ambassador of New York Tourism" and crowned the Spokesperson for "The Times Square Survival Guide." NAKED COWBOY also officially became *the most photographed person in the world* at the end of 2007. Naked Cowboy ran for mayor of NYC in 2009 and he is also the Grand Marshal of NYC's famous Underwear Run as part of the NYC marathon.

In 2010, I negotiated Naked Cowboy's biggest endorsement deal to date with Chris Quartuccio of Blue Island Shellfish Farms to harvest "Naked Cowboy Oysters" from Long Island Sound and distribute them live to fine restaurants worldwide. Naked Cowboy Oysters are now the best selling oysters in New York City and can be found at fine restaurants worldwide. Robert Burck increased his political aspirations and on October sixth, 2010 he announced his candidacy for President of The United States, hoping to lead the Tea Party to the White House.

CPSIA information can be obtained
at www.ICGtesting.com
Printed in the USA
BVOW08s0246191216
471211BV00002B/256/P

9 780557 964680